The Complete Handbook of

PRUNING

The Complete Handbook of
PRUNING

Brian Halliwell
Assistant Curator, Royal Botanic Gardens, Kew

John Turpin
B. Sc. (Hort)

John Wright
B. Sc. (Hort) N.D.H.

Ward Lock Limited · London

© Ward Lock Limited 1973, 1979

First published in Great Britain in 1973
by Ward Lock Limited, 116 Baker Street,
London W1M 2BB,
a Pentos Company

Second Edition 1979

Text filmset in Plantin

Printed and bound by Butler & Tanner Ltd

British Library Cataloguing in Publication Data

Halliwell, Brian, b. 1929
    The complete handbook of pruning.—2nd ed.
    1. Pruning
    I. Title. II. Halliwell, Brian   III. Turpin, John
    IV. Wright, John
    635′.04′42   SB125
    ISBN 0–7063–5781–7

Contents

Acknowledgements

With the exception of the figures cited below, all line drawings are by John Roberts: Fig. 5.7; Fig. 8.1 (after *The Fruit Garden Displayed*, pp. 59–60, published by Royal Horticultural Society); Fig. 9.1 (after *The Fruit Garden Displayed*, p. 91); Fig. 10.1; Fig. 11.1 (after *The Complete Guide to Fruit and Vegetable Growing*, p. 107, copyright George Rainbird Ltd.); Fig. 12.2 (also after *The Complete Guide to Fruit and Vegetable Growing*, p. 104).

The publishers gratefully acknowledge Donald Smith for granting permission to reproduce the colour photograph of raspberry canes on p. 123.

Publisher's Note

In this second edition, Brian Halliwell was responsible for the revision of the text for Chapters 1–7, 13, 14 and 16; John Wright was responsible for revising the text for Chapters 8–12.

Introduction

To prune or not to prune? This is a question that always seems to face gardeners. Most feel they ought, but are not sure why or how. It is accepted practice for the orchard, fairly frequently carried out in the rose garden but rather haphazardly elsewhere. Most often it is only performed when a shrub or tree begins to encroach on its neighbour, a path or a building.

Pruning is often looked upon as the answer to make a barren tree fruitful. Carried out correctly, it will—eventually! Years of neglect cannot be rectified in one season. The unknowing pruner who cuts because he thinks he ought but does not know how, often finishes up with no flowers at all through too hard pruning or carrying out the operation at the wrong time of year.

Some gardeners are obsessed by tidiness and formality, wanting their trees and shrubs to be like smart soldiers on parade. Trees are lopped to a standard height, whilst for shrubs out come the clippers and branches and twigs are cut back to a predetermined size and shape all identical. As spring advances, the gardener becomes distraught for he has not allowed for the different angles or rates of growth that now reduce his parade-ground effect to a shambles. Strict uniformity is in any case acceptable only in the parterre which is laid out in symmetrical geometric designs where lines have to be kept sharp.

What then is pruning? Why does one prune? When? How?

Pruning can be described as the removal of a part or parts of a woody plant by man for specific purpose. The reasons for pruning are:

1 To train the plant
2 To maintain plant health
3 To obtain a balance between growth and flowering
4 To improve the quality of flowers, fruit, foliage or stems
5 To restrict growth

Training

A woody plant will come into cropping earlier if it is allowed to grow naturally. Pruning delays flowering but in the early years it ensures a framework of strong well-spaced branches, later to produce flowers and fruit. A tree of desired size and shape can be fashioned which is not only well balanced and delightful to the eye but carries flowers or fruits where they can be easily seen and reached. Building up of the initial framework makes for easier management of tree, shrub or climber in later years.

Maintenance of plant health

A beautiful tree is a healthy one! Control of pests and diseases is essential and it is easiest if the cause of these afflictions can be removed as early as possible. Pruning is one way in which this can be done. In early years, pests and diseases interfere with training; in an aged specimen they hasten the end; whilst at all stages of growth they are unsightly, can destroy flowers or fruit and weaken branches—the fall of a large branch can mean severe damage or death to the tree.

Routine spraying can control pests and some diseases in shrubs and young trees but it becomes impracticable if not impossible on large trees, when pruning is the only feasible method of control. Most diseases that attack trees enter through wounds and spread via the conducting tissue, killing off branches as they extend their hold. If disease reaches the trunk death usually results. The disease organism travels beyond the wood it has killed and its presence in apparently healthy wood can be

7

detected by a brown interior staining. When diseased wood is being removed always cut back to sound wood, that is, wood where there is no staining.

Dead wood is always unsightly and likely to break off, causing damage. It is the breeding ground for disease which can spread from the dead wood to the live (eg coral spot). When removing any wood include also that which is dead.

Maintaining a balance between growth and flowering

A tree or shrub in strong active growth produces few flowers and in fact too heavy pruning can delay or even prevent flowering. Pruning in the early years should be sufficient only for training.

Once a tree has come into full flowering, shoot production will decline until at maturity very little annual growth is being added. In a mature plant it is the young wood which produces leaves and in many plants even the flowers, whilst with age the quality of these and the rate at which they are produced declines. It is therefore desirable to encourage a woody plant to maintain the production of young wood by judicious pruning.

Improvement of quality of flowers, fruit, foliage and stems

The more flowers and fruit a plant produces, the smaller they become, as can be witnessed on an unpruned rosebush or fruit tree. Pruning reduces the amount of wood and so diverts energy into the production of larger, though fewer, flowers and/or fruit. The length of flower spikes on an unpruned butterfly bush *Buddleia davidii* may be 10cm (4in) but can exceed 30cm (1ft) on one that has been hard pruned.

Leaves are produced only on current season's growth. The more vigorous this is the larger will be the leaves, and in plants with coloured leaves the more intense will be the colouring. Shrubs grown for their foliage, summer or autumn, variegated, coloured or dissected, are pruned hard annually.

Some deciduous shrubs have coloured barks which are especially delightful in winter. The best colour is produced on young stems and the greatest length and most intense colour results from hard pruning.

Restriction of growth

Trees and shrubs left to develop naturally grow bigger and bigger, becoming an embarrassment where space is restricted and so pruning becomes necessary to keep them within bounds.

Other forms of pruning

There are some jobs carried out in a garden which are also forms of pruning although they are not always recognised as such. The cutting of flowers from woody plants for home decoration is a type of pruning. Trimming of hedges is restrictive pruning applied to a row of shrubs. Topiary, the clipping of bushes to bizarre shapes, is a combination of training and restrictive pruning, and so is pleaching, used to make living screens or arches. Tree surgery is an extreme form of pruning to maintain a mature tree in a healthy condition.

For the gardener pruning is essentially an artificial operation and he may well question its necessity when it does not occur in nature. But it does! Some shrubs and trees not only shed leaves annually but they also shed twigs, as in *Tamarix* and dawn redwood *Metasequoia glyptostroboides*. Eucalyptus saplings produce a thicket of shoots from which the strongest grow away at the expense of the remainder to become the leaders; the rest die. Later a long clean trunk is produced by the natural shedding of branches.

Weather conditions such as wind, drought and frost (and, of course, fire) can remove portions of plants, usually the growing points; this affects development and the trees become shrub-like. Animals, as distinct from man, feed on young growth and often remove these succulent growing points so that trees fail to develop a single stem but produce many, thus remaining as shrubs. In Africa the opposite process occurs: herbivores turn large shrubs into trees by feeding on young growth of the side branches and leaving the woody and unpalatable main stems untouched, so producing an arborescent effect. Pests and diseases can also play a part in the natural pruning process, often by destroying the growing points.

THE PRUNING OF ORNAMENTAL PLANTS

1 Training by Pruning

Most trees and shrubs grown in a garden are purchased from a nursery. It is useful for the reader to know how these were raised for it does have some bearing on pruning.

Woody plants may be on their own roots, having been raised from seed, cuttings or layers; or they may have a root system (root-stock) of one plant and the aerial part (scion) of another as a result of grafting (budding is but one form of grafting). Grafting is used to propagate trees and shrubs because:

1 It is the most reliable or only method of increase
2 By use of a selected rootstock it is possible to regulate the ultimate size of tree, eg as in fruit trees
3 It is possible to produce artificial types of trees, eg shrubs can be made into trees or pendulous shrubs can become weeping standards
4 It can induce earlier flowering, eg grafted tree magnolias flower earlier than those raised from seed

Trees may be grafted low, with their union close to the ground, or they may be high grafted on to stems of varying lengths. When planting, those that are grafted low should have their union buried unless the rootstock governs the ultimate size of the tree, as with flowering crabs on apple rootstocks; these are planted with their union well above ground-level.

Remember that grafted trees and shrubs are always likely to produce suckers from their rootstocks, and these, if left, grow away at the expense of the scion variety. Suckers should be removed as soon as they appear. Do not cut off at ground-level otherwise all buds below will start into growth and where there was one sucker there will now be several. Scrape away the soil until the point of origin is exposed, then with a sharp downward pull remove the sucker; this takes away the basal buds which cutting would have left.

Rooted cuttings, layers and graded seedlings are lined out in nursery rows and grown on for a year, by which time some of the shrubs may be ready for selling. The rest of the shrubs and the trees are grown on until ready for sale.

Deciduous trees

These may be sold as whips which have a single straight stem and perhaps a few feathers, which are short side branches an inch or two in length (Fig. 1.1). Whips are relatively cheap even if they are small, but they do allow maximum scope for training. They are sold bare-rooted and should be planted in the garden to the same depth as in the nursery; planting can be done during open weather at any time from October till March: staking may be necessary.

In the nursery or in your garden, these whips put on extension growth from the apical bud with development of feathers or side branches along the length of the main stem. These can all be retained for they help to thicken the main stem even if they slow down apical development. If all are removed, there is a greater increase in length of the leader but the main stem remains thin. An intermediate process known as feathering is often adopted. All side branches or feathers on the lowest third of the tree are removed; on the second third all side branches are reduced to two or three buds, whilst the top third is left unpruned except to remove any upright branch which is challenging the leader (Figs. 1.2 & 1.3). This practice continues annually until there is a sufficient length of trunk, and then the branching system is allowed to develop. Such pruning is usually done in winter while the tree is dormant.

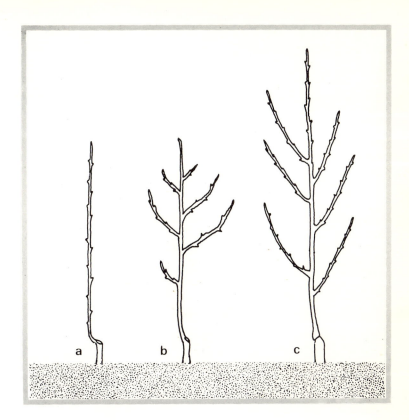

Fig. 1.1. Types of fruit trees as usually purchased: (a) a whip; (b) a feathered whip; (c) a whip in its second year

Trees are trained in two main ways: as standards which have a clear 1·8m (6ft) stem from the top of which the framework is allowed to develop; and as central leaders where the leader is continuous, with branches arising all the way along the length of trunk.

Standards

When the young leader reaches about 2·25m (7½ft) the tip is removed to encourage branching. Again, this operation is usually carried out in winter. This produces a tree (Fig. 1.4a) with a clear 1·8m (6ft) trunk (a half-standard has a clear 1·05m (3½ft) stem). Standards are the form commonly offered for sale by nurseries and are well suited to small-growing trees such as crab apples and mountain ash. But for the larger-growing trees the central leader should be used.

Central leaders

Instead of being stopped, the leader is allowed to grow unchecked, and in the nursery branches are allowed to develop at 1·8m (6ft) from the ground (Fig. 1.4b). When the gardener is training, a clear stem of 2·4m (8ft) is preferable to allow mowing beneath in comfort; if he has purchased the tree from the nursery with a clear stem of only 1·8m (6ft) this can easily be rectified. The length of clear stem to aim for depends, of course, on the kind of tree and the general habit of growth. In a number of trees branches become partly pendulous with age and sweep downwards; such trees are better with a trunk of 4·5m (15ft) or even more to keep branches clear of the ground. When branches are allowed to develop, they should be spaced at intervals along the length of the trunk. At the same time aim to produce a well-balanced head by allowing branches to develop only at planned points around the circumference. If a tree throws two leading shoots, remove one (Fig. 1.5).

Maidens

Grafted trees in their first year grow away very strongly, making anything up to 2·7m (9ft) of growth. These are usually clear stems, though they may also have feathers, and are called maidens, being sometimes sold as such. They are trained in exactly the same way as has been described for standards and central leaders.

11

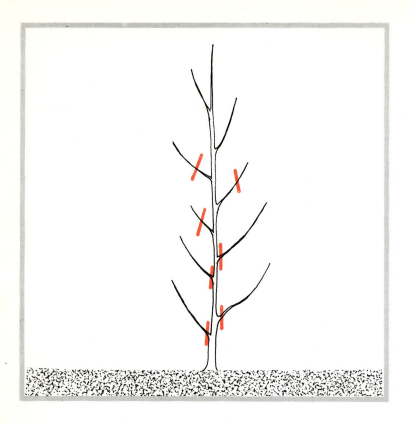

Fig. 1.2. Treatment of a feathered whip, one year after planting

Fig. 1.3. Treatment in following year

12

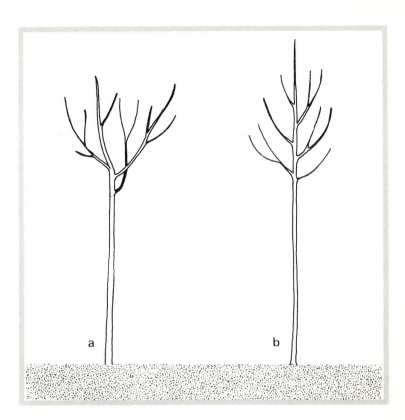

Fig. 1.4. (a) Standard tree where leading shoot has been pinched out at 2m (6ft); (b) A young tree with a central leader

Fig. 1.5. A double leader resulting from a tree producing two leaders of equal vigour; remove the one on the right

a

Fig. 1.6. Increasing the height
of the leader of a pendulous
tree which has been high
worked.
(a) First winter

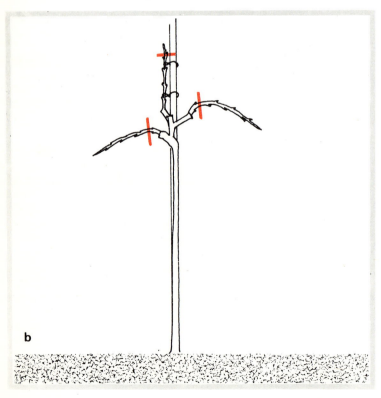

b

(b) Second winter

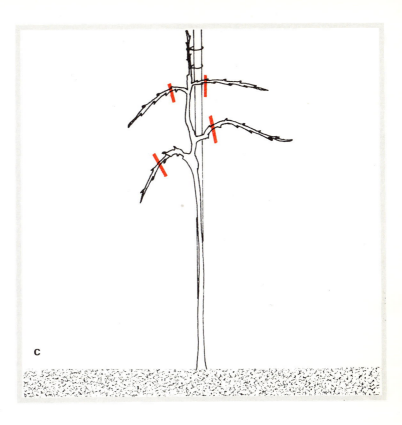

(c) Third winter

Pendulous trees

A few of these, eg weeping willows, can be raised from cuttings. A single leader is selected, feathered and supported, and sold by the nursery in varying lengths of stem. On planting in the garden, secure the main stem to a long stout pole, 3·6m (12ft) high if possible, and train the leader up this, feathering annually. When the top of the pole is reached, the main framework can be trained in.

Pendulous forms of normally upright trees—eg beech, ash, elm—are grafted. They may be grafted low which is to be preferred when the leader is tied to a stake and feathered. Most often they are high grafted on to stems of 6ft and upwards. When planted in the garden, the leader should be cut back to where it is bending over and all other branches reduced. Select the strongest shoot and train upwards securing to a 3·6m (12ft) stake (Fig. 1.6). When the top has been reached, a framework can be trained in and after the crown has attained sufficient proportion the natural weeping habit can be allowed. This will produce a graceful tree with plenty of height for the hanging branches. When pendulous branches are allowed to form on top of a 1·8m (6ft) or 2·4m (8ft) stem the result is squat and ugly.

In some forms of pendulous tree the leader continues its upward development without the necessity of being tied to a support.

Evergreen trees

In the nursery evergreens are allowed to develop with a central leader but all side shoots are retained. Sold as either container-grown or balled, they should be planted in the garden, in a position protected from wind, and staked. Planting is best carried out in spring. Retain the central leader and the side branches as long as possible, although some trimming of these, and some thinning where crowded is beneficial, and this, again, should be done in spring. As with deciduous trees, the main branches are not allowed to form under a height of 2·4m (8ft) from the ground, and crowded and crossing branches are removed and so are double leaders. If trees have attractive barks, as in some species of *Arbutus*, feather the leader to expose the trunk as soon as possible.

15

Conifers

These are allowed to grow naturally in the nursery, apart from the removal of surplus leaders, until they reach the size at which they will be sold. When planted in the garden, the single leader should be retained, any leader competition being removed in spring, and also any branches low down on the tree which begin to grow away strongly. Most conifers should be allowed to retain their side branches as long as possible; they should not be removed until they die naturally. An exception might be made with those trees having a naturally pendulous habit for if all the branches are left on the lower part an unsightly clutter results.

Do now allow the main framework to develop too low down on the tree. The first main branch should not be allowed below 2·4m (8ft) from ground-level. Conifers with pendulous branches should not be allowed to develop their main branches under 3·6m (12ft) so that they will sweep down towards the ground gracefully. Conifers such as the *Chamaecyparis* cultivars may develop several leaders which in their early years may be unnoticed and cause no trouble for they grow vertically and close together so that the desired shape is maintained. But as the trees age the trunks begin to fall outwards under the weight of their side branches and so spoil the outline. To correct this condition the trunks must be tied together. This need not happen if one keeps only a single leader, although with certain fastigiate forms such as the Irish yew (*Taxus baccata* 'Fastigiata') several leaders have to be trained, and tying in of these at a later date is necessary.

Some conifers remain shrub-like, eg *Cephalotaxus* and some of the forms of yew (*Taxus*), and these have several leaders. They can be allowed to develop naturally, being occasionally trimmed to shape or to restrict growth. Dwarf or small-growing conifers, too, are left to develop naturally even if they have a multiplicity of leaders.

It is important that conifers having a tiered habit, eg pines, firs and spruces, should retain only a single leader. Leaders can be damaged by animals, pests, or the weather, but should this happen a group of new leaders will develop of which the straightest and strongest only should be retained.

Pruning of conifers should be carried out when fully dormant otherwise excessive gumming can occur if branches are cut when the sap is rising.

Training shrubs

Deciduous specimens

Sold most often in nurseries as bare-rooted, these should be soaked in water prior to firm planting to the same depth as in the nursery. Grafted specimens should be planted with their union just below ground-level. Following planting, select and retain three or five of the strongest shoots, cutting back side shoots to two or three buds and reducing their length by about half. This should encourage new shoots to develop near to ground-level in the following growing season; in the next winter these stems are cut back again to half of their new growth. At the same time the centre of the bush is opened up by removing crossing branches and any clutter of short shoots. Cut back the remaining side shoots to two or three buds and thin where crowded so as to produce a well-balanced, evenly spaced framework.

Evergreens

Sold either as balled specimens or as container-grown, these are planted in April to the same depth as they were in the nursery, having first been given a good soaking. Select the three strongest shoots and lightly tip or remove their growing points; reduce the remainder. In the following April, thin out crowded branches and open up the centre of the bush.

Tender shrubs

Most often sold in containers, they are best planted in May after the danger of frost has passed. Ensure that plants from containers are not root-bound otherwise they will be slow to establish and will rarely anchor well, always being liable to blow out of the ground, especially when they produce large tops. Deciduous subjects should have their shoots reduced by half and their side shoots cut back to two or three buds. In the following May repeat the process, thinning out and opening up the centre of the bush. Evergreens should be lightly tipped or have the growing point removed after planting. In the following May, thin and open up the centre of the bush.

2 Pruning of Established Trees and Shrubs

As an annual operation and prior to any kind of pruning a number of basic tasks must be performed. All dead, damaged and diseased wood, and suckers at their point of origin, must be removed from grafted plants. Crossing branches, thin and crowded shoots should be cut out. Shoots which are showing reversion, a common complaint with the foliage of variegated plants and an occasional occurrence with flower colour, eg in camellias, should have the offending branch traced back to its point of origin and removed. All these tasks should be carried out in the spring.

Procedure for established trees

Once a tree has received its initial training pruning becomes negligible, although any strong branch which develops from low down on the tree, any growing near to the vertical and leader competition should be removed. Carry out on deciduous trees in winter whilst dormant and on evergreens in late March just before growth commences. The central leader will decrease in vigour over the years until it ceases to be a leader, whilst the crown will become more rounded or flattened. At all times the aim should be to maintain the outline of the crown and any branch that spoils this should be reduced or removed. Ensure that main branches are spaced evenly along the length of the trunk without too many developing from one small area. Periodical shortening of limbs may be advisable to reduce the possibilities of damage in gales, but problems of large dangerous limbs, bracing, propping or tree felling should be referred to a qualified tree surgeon (*see also* page 139).

Trees growing in restricted areas need regular attention to prevent encroachment. This should be carried out when they are fully dormant, offending branches being cut back to a point where a younger side branch originates. Remove some of the oldest branches each year. Aim to continually train in young main branches so that old wood can be removed entirely. Do not in desperation hack the main branches back so that all that remains of the tree is the trunk with the bases of limbs! Too often one sees this kind of treatment meted out to street trees and nothing looks more hideous, especially in the winter months.

Some trees, eg limes, develop twiggy growth along the length of their trunk and this can spoil their appearance. These shoots should be removed regularly by rubbing them off whilst they are still soft or by cutting off carefully when they become woody. A chemical is now available which if sprayed or painted on the trunk will prevent or drastically reduce the appearance of such growths.

Pruning of established shrubs

The method and timing of pruning deciduous shrubs is governed by the age of the wood on which flowering takes place: this may be on current season's growth, on one-year-old wood or spurs. Evergreens and tender plants are considered separately, and so also is pruning carried out for a special effect.

Shrubs flowering on current season's growth

Growth has to be made before flowering can take place so shrubs within this group tend to flower in summer and autumn. If left unpruned, shrubs grow higher but with reduced vigour, more flowers are produced but these are smaller and poorer in quality. Hard

Fig. 2.1. The pruning of shrubs which flower on the current season's growth. The object is to remove those shoots which have already flowered

pruning means the removal of a large amount of wood so that the energy of the bush is diverted to fewer shoots and flowers which are consequently larger and of better quality.

Pruning is carried out when bushes are dormant, during the period from December to March. Weather permitting, January or February are the best months. All shoots are cut back hard to within two or three buds of ground-level or a framework (Fig. 2.1).

Another method is to cut half the shoots back to two or three buds and the remainder to a half or third of their length. Hard pruning delays flowering but with this treatment the flowering period can be extended and the quality of flowers is still high. The following winter these longer shoots are removed completely; some thinning of resultant shoots is beneficial in May.

When shrubs of this nature flower in flushes or flower continuously, dead-heading should be practised to improve their appearance and to prevent them expending energy on ripening fruit. This consists of the removal of the dead flower and if possible two or three buds on the flower stem; cutting is to be preferred, for

though some stems can be easily broken off, others sustain damage to neighbouring buds.

Strong growth and good quality flowers following hard pruning depend upon plentiful food supply, so apply a base dressing of a general fertilizer at the rate of 68–136g/sq m (2–4oz/sq yd) the heavier dressing for old and well-established shrubs.

Shrubs flowering on one-year-old wood

Growth is made in one growing season and in the following year flowers are produced either on this growth or on short laterals coming from it. This group tends to flower in the early part of the year from January until May. Individual shrubs can be pruned directly after flowering, or pruning can be delayed until July when all the shrubs in the garden falling within this group can be treated; if berries are to be a feature pruning takes place in March (Fig. 2.2).

Shrubs in this group can be left unpruned but they tend to become too tall, encroach on their neighbours or create an unmanageable tangle of growth. Pruning then consists of removing the twigs which have flowered. If

Fig. 2.2. The pruning of shrubs which flower on one-year-old wood. The shoot which has flowered is removed, leaving the new growth to flower the following season

young growth is breaking, cut back to where there is a strong young shoot growing in the desired direction. Thin out the remainder of the shoots, especially opening up the centre of the bush so as to improve air movement which will help to ripen wood. Unripe wood is especially a problem during a wet season when growth is lush. In August of such a year, carry out a further thinning to help ripen wood; a light dressing of sulphate of potash is also beneficial. As less wood is removed in the pruning of this group smaller applications of a general fertilizer are required. This can be at the rate of 34–68g/sq m (1–2oz/sq yd) annually, or double the rate every second year.

Shrubs flowering on spurs

A spur can be described as a branch, usually a short one, which will produce its flower buds on one-year-old wood but will continue each year to produce more on the same branch; sometimes the wood has to be two years old before flower buds are produced but new flower buds continue to be added in subsequent years. These shrubs grow strongly in their early years, producing few flowers, but as growth slows down, so spurs begin to form naturally and there is a reduction of extension growth. When this stage is reached, pruning can almost cease.

Pruning may need to be practised during the early years of development, especially if space is limited. Once a framework has been formed all annual stems are cut back to three or four buds, with the exception of the leading shoot on main branches. The following growing season some of these buds will grow away, the others will form flower buds to produce blossom in the next year. Once these flower buds form, any growth which develops beyond them should be removed.

Evergreens

Their main attraction in the garden is their foliage in the winter months. Most evergreens are liable to damage if exposed to cold winds or subject to prolonged low temperatures when the ground stays frozen for long periods. This shows itself by death of branches or the discoloration and death of leaves. Pruning of evergreens is carried out in April just before growth commences. Cut out any winter-damaged

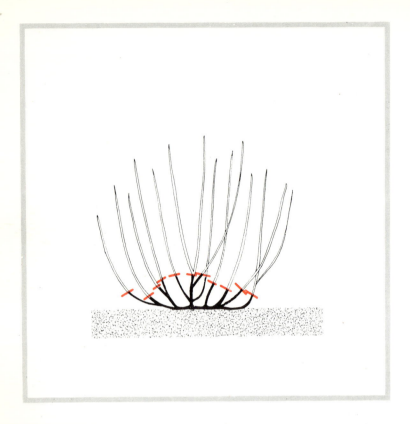

Fig. 2.3. Specialized pruning for bark effect. As the brightest colour is produced on strong young shoots, all growth is cut back hard at bud burst in spring. Used on some kinds of *Cornus* and *Salix*

wood, trimming back discoloured foliage; thin and trim to shape. If evergreens are also grown for their flowers, they invariably produce these on one-year wood and so pruning is delayed until after flowering.

Tender plants
As these are always liable to damage by frost pruning is delayed until May when the danger of severe frost has passed. Those flowering on one-year-old wood are not pruned until after flowering. Pruning consists of the removal of winter damage, removal of stalks which have carried flowers and some thinning.

Pruning for special effects
Shrubs are not always grown in gardens for flowers and fruit; sometimes stems or bark or leaves have more appeal.

Shrubs such as the *Cornus alba* forms or the coloured osiers (*Salix alba* forms) are planted for the effect of their colourful bark during the winter months. Bark colour is most intense on young wood and the best effect is from the strong young shoots that result from hard pruning (Fig. 2.3). Species of *Rubus* and *Cornus* that sucker and any other shrubs with a similar habit can be cut down to ground-level in March. Those which do not have this habit are treated rather differently. Several leaders are permitted, each of which is feathered so as to expose the lower part of the stems.

Ailanthus altissima (tree of heaven) has large compound leaves which are attractive, but as it makes a tree 18m (60ft) in height this is obviously too large a subject for a small garden. The young plants, however, make very strong growth in their early years and on these strong unbranched shoots are even larger leaves; this habit can be retained if shoots are cut down to ground-level annually in March and fed copiously.

Many shrubs have more attractive foliage, either summer or autumn, than flowers. Leaves are only produced on current season's growth and those of the largest size are on the strongest growth. Deciduous shrubs with variegated, coloured or cut foliage are pruned hard almost to ground-level or to a framework during the winter months and fed copiously.

Removing a large limb from a mature tree. Firstly a cut is made at some distance from the main stem, and the weight of the branch removed. If any tearing occurs it will not affect the final pruned surface. The stump of the branch is then removed flush with the main stem, and the cut surface pared with a pruning knife until it is smooth. Finally the wound is painted with a pruning compound, which prevents diseases entering the exposed wood and acts as a temporary bark until the tree's own bark grows across the wound.

Pruning a rambler rose. The first picture shows the unpruned rose at the end of a season's growth. It is then completely removed from its support, laid out on the ground, pruned, and then tied back into position.

Pruning a bush rose of moderately vigorous habit. The first picture shows the unpruned rose, the final one the finished result.

3 Climbers and Wall Shrubs

Climbers are plants with weak stems that take themselves up towards the light by means of their climbing habit. Plants have adapted themselves to this habit in a number of different ways:

1 by twining stems, as in the common honeysuckle *Lonicera periclymenum*,
2 by twining leaf stalks, as in clematis,
3 by tendrils, as with the vines *Vitis* species,
4 by tendrils producing pads that stick to their supports, as in the Virginia creeper *Parthenocissus tricuspidata*,
5 by roots produced on aerial stems which stick to their support, the best example being the common ivy *Hedera helix*,
6 by thorns which hook on to support, as in climbing roses.

In addition there are plants, lax of habit, that get themselves up to the light by flopping over rocks, trees or other shrubs.

In the garden climbers can be used for a number of purposes: for covering pergolas, walls and fences; for training up poles; and for growing over or through trees and shrubs. One chooses the climber most suitable for a particular site. On a bare wall or fence only a climber that sticks itself to its support can be used, but if the wall is provided with a trellis or parallel wires almost any kind of climber can be grown.

Supports for climbers

Trellises should be securely fixed in position after having been painted or treated with wood preservative prior to erection. The thickness of timber to be used depends on the type of plant it has to support. Strong climbers such as wisteria produce heavy stems, so strong supports are necessary. Metal trellising can be used as

long as it has been painted or galvanized and, again, the heaviest gauge is necessary for the strongest climbers. If climbers are going to be grown against wooden buildings or fences that will need painting periodically, it is advisable to fix the trellises to their support with hinges so that they can be swung away at painting times.

Parallel wires are quite suitable and easier than trellising to install and maintain; they should be of a sufficiently heavy gauge to support the climbers and galvanized, painted or covered with plastic. Fix them to the wall horizontally, with 23–30cm (9–12in) between them, through eyebolts with strainers at each end to keep the wires taut. Upright canes, vertical strings or wires are often added to give extra support.

Trees make admirable supports for strong-growing climbers. The trees should be mature, but even dead trees can be used; in fact if there is a dead or unsightly tree in the garden which cannot be removed, the best thing to do is to hide it under a climber. Dead trees should have their smaller branches removed, and with live trees it is advisable to reduce the canopy to admit more light. After planting the climber insert a cane or fix vertical wires to take the stems up into the branches of the tree.

Pergolas again need strong climbers that get their stems up on top of the structure as quickly as possible. The reduced light from the top cover causes lower leaves to fall, resulting in bare stems near to ground-level, but selected small climbers can be planted in to hide the bareness and introduce colour lower down.

Supporting poles may be of trimmed timber, cut tree branches or metal. Wooden poles need to be treated with wood preservative, at least at their bases, and metal posts must be painted or galvanized to prevent rusting. Grow the weaker climbers on poles, or be sure to prune each year so that there is never more growth than the poles can support.

When shrubs are to act as supports, choose those that are well established, reasonably vigorous and of moderate size. Select climbers which are not themselves of vigorous growth and be prepared to be ruthless with them at pruning time so that the supporting shrub is not smothered.

Preparation of site for climbers

At the foot of walls, fences and pergolas the soil is usually poor and often contains large amounts of builder's rubble, all of which should be removed. Near a house wall there may be drains or underground pipes and it is advisable to know their positions. Dig over the soil, incorporating as much organic matter as possible; thorough preparation is essential prior to planting to provide optimum conditions for growth. The soil at the base of walls, fences and pergolas receives little rain and remains relatively dry. Never plant your climber less than 9–12in away from a wall, and water new plantings until well established.

Soil at the base of trees and shrubs is also poor, so to ensure quick establishment take out a hole 30–45cm (12–18in) deep, fill with fresh soil and organic matter and plant into this. Here, too, the soil is dry, with little rain reaching it naturally and the tree or shrub competing for what there is; so, again, water after planting until the climber is established.

Planting climbers

Climbers are now almost always container-grown and on sale throughout the year. April planting is the best, but planting can be done throughout much of the year as long as attention is paid to watering until the climber is established. After planting, reduce the stems to a half or even a third of their original lengths to encourage young growth to develop at or near ground-level. Select three or five of the strongest shoots, provide them with canes, vertical wires or strings, and train them in the desired direction of the permanent support. At the end of the next growing season reduce all the leaders by about a half, cutting the weakest shoots even harder; thin out crowded shoots and space well the main stems. Repeat each year until the allotted space has been filled with a well-spaced framework.

Regular attention is necessary in the training of climbers, and when growth is in spate they need almost daily attention. Clematis and other plants that have twining leaf stalks, if neglected even for a week, produce an unmanageable tangle which defies the patience of Job to unravel. Moreover, if climbers that stick to their supports either by roots or sucker pads are allowed to wander in the wrong direction, it means that the shoots must be pulled off whatever surface they have fastened on and they will not stick again.

Evergreens are treated similarly to deciduous climbers but pruning is always less severe, the growth being tipped rather than cut hard back. Do ensure that the bases of walls and fences are adequately clothed to start with and keep them so.

Established pruning for climbers

The same rules apply to established pruning for climbers as for shrubs, that is the method and timing is dependent on the age of the wood on which flowers are produced. Those which flower on current season's growth can be cut hard back to an established framework during the winter; more often they are cut to ground-level. When pruned hard, flowering is delayed, but the flowering season may be extended by leaving in some shoots which are trimmed but not cut hard; these are removed completely in the following year. Very late flowering climbers in this group, or in areas where early frosts are prevalent, are cut much less severely, with growth being reduced by about half and this removed completely in the following winter.

Climbers flowering on previous season's wood are pruned after flowering. Shoots which have flowered are removed or cut back to where new growth is developing, and thinning out of remaining growth follows. Train in new shoots as they develop, keeping only enough to comfortably furnish; any surplus should be removed.

After a framework has been formed, the spur

producers have all side shoots cut back to two or three buds during February. For some this treatment may have to be carried out twice, once in July when shoots are cut to four or five buds and again in February when any resulting growth is shortened back to two or three.

Climbers on poles need drastic pruning at all times, irrespective of the group to which they belong, to ensure that no more growth is permitted than the poles can support. Climbers on trees, on the other hand, need no further pruning once they are established, unless growth becomes excessive and threatens the tree or if a clutter of dead wood occurs. On pergolas pruning is minimal, just thinning out to prevent overcrowding and removing shoots which wave about in the wind and annoy people passing beneath. Some training in of young growth should be practised so that periodically some of the oldest stems can be removed.

Siting and planting of wall shrubs

An area close to a wall is more protected than one in the open, and of course drier. In summer walls absorb as well as reflect heat and so, being warm and dry, help to ripen wood.

A south wall is the warmest and driest and well suited to growing plants considered to be tender or needing to have their wood thoroughly ripened to flower freely. A west wall is almost as good. An east wall, however, is not suitable for early flowering shrubs; flowers of many plants can withstand some freezing without damage as long as they can thaw out slowly, but winter or early spring flowers are likely to be damaged in the early morning sunshine on an east wall. Such a wall is better suited for the growing of sprawling or climbing plants than for plants considered to be tender.

On a north wall there is no direct sun, and so it remains moister with less fluctuation of temperature, hence cooler than a more open position. A north wall, therefore, is well suited to shade lovers and shrubs requiring cool, moist growing conditions in summer.

When there are south or west walls in the garden it is possible to be more adventurous in the choice of plants and to try out trees or shrubs which are classed as tender in a particular district for growing in the open. Shrubs which, when grown in the open, flower sparsely or not at all, especially after a wet summer when wood fails to ripen properly, often flower profusely against a wall. West and south walls offer protection to shrubs that flower in winter months by allowing flowers to develop fully and remain open and undamaged by the cold.

Shrubs for planting against a wall may be offered bare-rooted, balled in the case of evergreens, but many and especially the tender ones, are now sold in containers. Planting is best carried out just before growth starts, which will be April for some of the deciduous shrubs but in most cases May planting is preferable. Plant firmly, 23–30cm (9–12in), away from the wall, and finish up with a shallow depression in the soil around the main stem so as to facilitate watering, which should continue until the shrubs are well established—on each occasion giving a good soaking.

Training wall shrubs

Wall plants which are naturally trees can be trained to a single leader. A single-stemmed young plant should be chosen and headed back in April to about 23cm (9in) above the lowest wire or 60cm (2ft) from the ground if on a trellis. Insert a strong cane or fix a vertical wire up which the leader is to be trained (Fig. 3.1a–b).

In the following growing season, the uppermost buds will develop. Select the strongest and train in as a new leader. Take the next two shoots and tie one on either side of the leader to canes fixed in position at an angle of 45° to the vertical; any surplus shoots are stopped at four buds. In the following April, lower the branches to an angle of 60° (keeping the side branches at an angle allows extension growth to develop). Meanwhile the leader is beheaded at 23cm (9in) above the next wire or about 45cm (18in) above the first pair of branches when growing on a trellis. The strongest shoot is again tied in as the leader, and two more are tied in at 45° whilst surplus shoots are stopped at four buds. In the following April again, the bottom pair of branches is brought to the horizontal, the second tier dropped to 60°, surplus shoots stopped at four buds and the leader again beheaded (Fig. 3.1c–g).

This practice continues until the uppermost

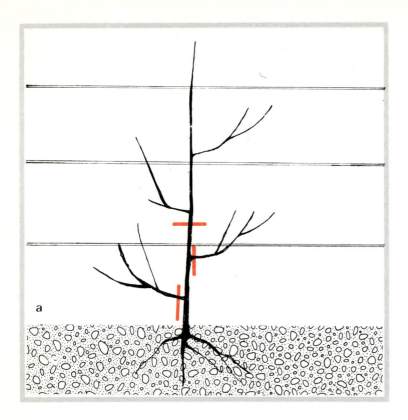

Fig. 3.1. Training a wall shrub
(a) First winter following planting, showing places for pruning cuts on two- or three-year-old bush

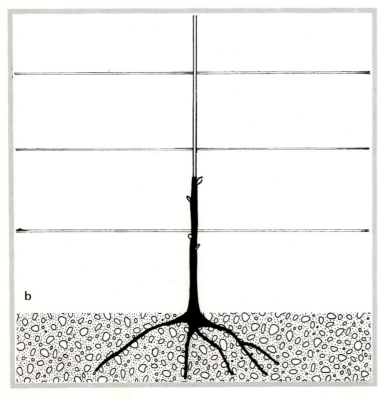

(b) After cuts

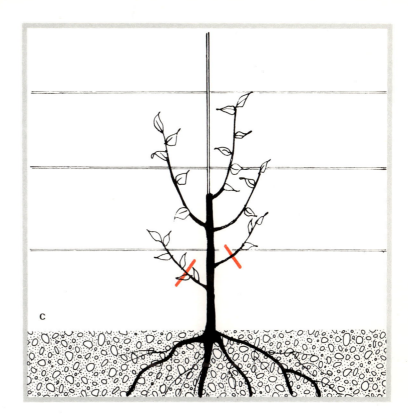

(c) Growth produced in first summer

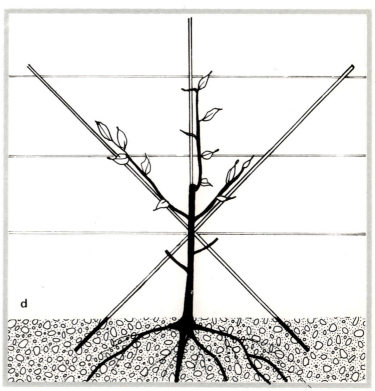

(d) Canes fixed in position at 45° to vertical. Lowest shoots cut back

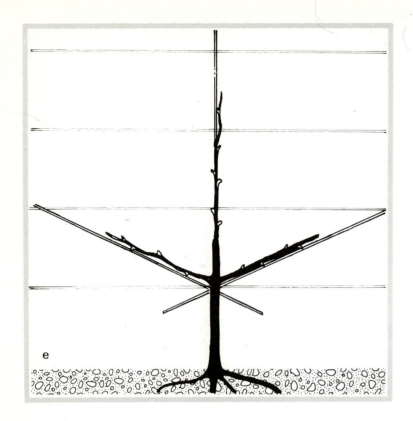

(e) Second winter. Canes lowered to 60° from vertical

(f) Second growing season showing second pair of canes fixed in position at 45° to vertical

28

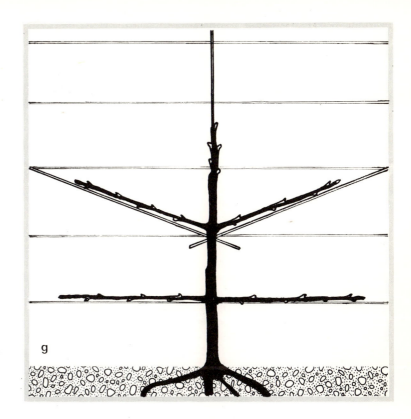

(g) Third winter. Lowest pair of branches lowered to horizontal. Second pair to 60° from vertical

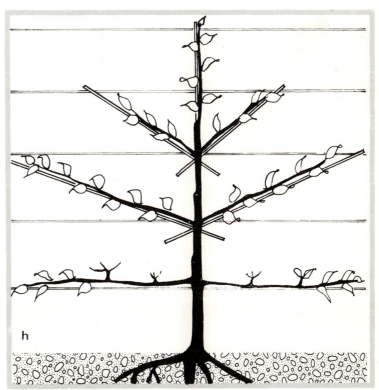

(h) Third growing season with third pair of canes fixed at 45° to vertical

wire or the top of the trellis is reached, after which the leader can be allowed to grow on. In July or August of the following year, the leader is then removed just above the top tier.

Once the bottom tier has been tied in horizontally, flowering can be allowed to take place. At all times any branches coming away from the wall are removed.

The above method may be slow but it builds up a well-balanced framework, provides good cover low down and flowering is progressive.

The following is a simpler method, best suited for deciduous subjects, and while not as good as the one just described it produces results more quickly and still provides reasonable cover (Fig. 3.2). On a single-stemmed young plant, cut a notch just above the buds that you wish to form branches during April. This forces those buds into growth which is allowed to develop untied whilst the leader is tied to a central cane or wire. In the following April or May, the best-placed side branches are pulled down towards the wire but not tied so tightly as to lie at the horizontal. Any surplus

shoots are cut back to two or three buds. Notch again above suitably placed buds with resulting shoots allowed to grow freely whilst the leader is secured to its vertical support. In the next year, prior to growth starting, the lowest branches resulting from the first year's notching are pulled down and tied at the horizontal. Those resulting from the previous year's notching are again tied loosely. This continues up to the top of the wall when the treatment of the leader as already described (page 25) is repeated.

Another method of training a tree, which is also well suited to most shrubs, is to produce a fan-trained framework. Plant a single-stemmed young plant and make a cut 90cm (3ft) from ground-level. Insert four canes, the lower pair at 45° and the upper at about 30° from the vertical. When growth starts, select the strongest four shoots and train up the canes, tying in at regular intervals. When planting a branched shrub select four stems and remove the remainder. Just prior to the commencement of the next growing sea-

a

Fig. 3.2. An alternative method of training a wall tree or shrub (a) Planting a maiden, first winter

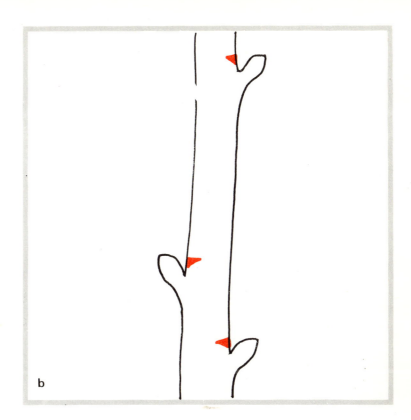

(b) A detail showing the position of the notches above each bud carried out in April

(c) Development of shoots from treated buds during the first summer

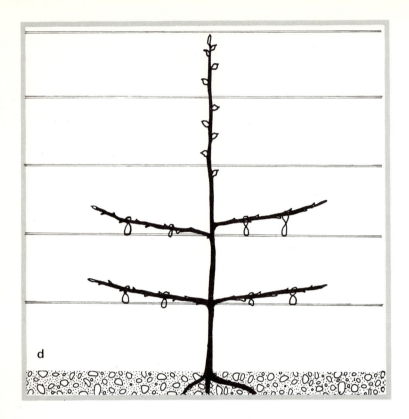

(d) Shoots pulled down and tied loosely in second winter

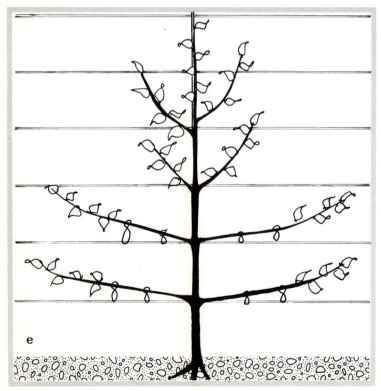

(e) Subsequent growth in second summer

32

(f) Second winter: lowest branches tied horizontally, upper pairs pulled down but tied loosely

son, cut back these four shoots to a third of their original length. Of the shoots produced, select two from each stem and tie to suitably fixed wires or strings, pinching back the remainder. At the end of the next growing season there will probably be a sufficient framework built up for shrubs, after which established pruning can begin.

Trees will need another season to complete the framework. Prior to the commencement of growth, all the leaders are reduced to about half of the length of wood produced in the previous season. Of the resulting growth select only two shoots, pinching back the remainder. Space these out and tie into position; if there are too many shoots any that are crowded can be removed completely. Now that the framework is complete, established pruning can commence.

Established pruning of wall shrubs

Tender shrubs and trees, especially ever-greens, are usually allowed to develop with the minimum of pruning. In May cut out any winter damage, thin out crowded shoots,

remove old flower stalks and cut back any shoots coming away from the wall. The same rules apply to tender shrubs as to all others, except that pruning is usually carried out later, that is, in May when the danger of frost has passed.

Deciduous trees and shrubs flowering on current season's growth can be cut hard back to the framework although sometimes some young stems are left unpruned apart from a light tipping.

The pruning of **deciduous trees and shrubs flowering on previous year's growth** is delayed until after flowering, when that growth which has flowered is removed, cutting back where possible to where new growth is breaking. Of the new growth, select only enough shoots to comfortably fill the available space and remove the rest. Those which are spur bearing will have all young shoots shortened back to two or three buds in July until a spur system has built up.

Irrespective of the type of pruning, periodically train in some new shoots into the framework so as to be able occasionally to remove some of the oldest wood.

33

4 Roses

Roses are occasionally raised on their own roots but in the main are grafted. Those on their own roots include a few climbers, shrubs or species roses raised from cuttings, though most species are raised from seed; in all of these shoots coming from below ground-level can be allowed to remain, for none will be suckers.

Removal of suckers

Most roses offered for sale are grafted, having a root system different from the aerial part of the plant. These roses may produce suckers and the gardener must be on the alert to deal with them. They usually arise from below ground-level, but this is not always the case with bushes that have been high planted so that the graft union is above soil-level. Equally, not all shoots rising from below ground-level need be suckers if bushes have been planted with their union below ground-level. Suckers on common bedding roses have smaller and more numerous leaflets than the rose variety, they are plain green, and either have no thorns or more numerous and smaller thorns. As there are several rootstocks in use for the commercial production of roses there is no one single type of sucker to watch for.

Whenever suckers are seen they should be removed; when they are small and young it is easier to do than when they are older and have become woody. Suckers should not be cut off at ground-level because this encourages subterranean buds to grow away and the result is several suckers in place of one. To deal with them effectually first scrape away the soil and expose their point of origin, then take the sucker in a gloved hand and pull sharply downwards; this removes both sucker and basal buds.

On standards, rub off any shoots which develop along the main stem and remove those that arise from below ground-level.

On species roses that are grafted it can be very difficult to detect suckers for there is a wider range of rootstocks used in their propagation and the suckers from some of these are very similar to the scion variety and difficult to identify.

Planting of roses

Container-grown roses, of recent introduction into Britain, mean that roses can be sold throughout the year. Although more expensive, they do allow the buyer to see just what he is buying, and planting can take place throughout much of the year, providing they are watered until established if in active growth.

The biggest demand, however, is still for bare-rooted roses which are offered for sale in the winter months (Fig. 4.1). Planting of these can safely take place at any time from leaf-fall until early April. See that the union is set just below soil-level, or if the roses are on their own roots plant them to the same depth as they were in the nursery.

Standard roses (Fig. 4.2) should be planted with a stake of sufficient strength to hold the rose tree firmly. Use a 1·2m (4ft) stake for half-standards, 1·8m (6ft) for full standards and 2·4m (8ft) for weeping standards. Wooden stakes should be painted or treated with a preservative and driven into the ground until the top is just below the graft union; secure twice, at about 23cm (9in) above the ground and just below the union. Weeping standards should be provided with a framework over which to train their weeping stems.

Fig. 4.1. Rose bush as bought from a nursery

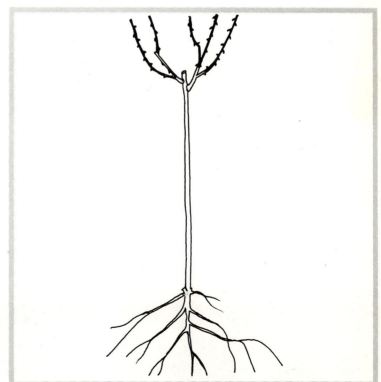

Fig. 4.2. A standard rose as bought from a nurseryman showing the point of union of the graft with the substantially greater root development usually found in standard roses as compared with bush roses

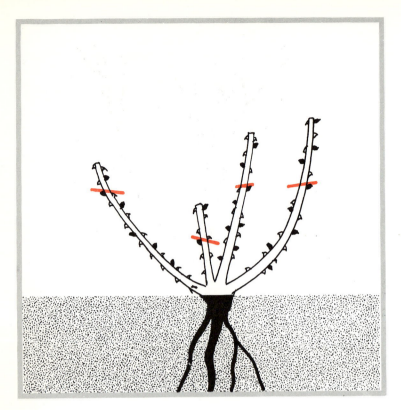

Fig. 4.3. Newly planted H.T. rose, showing just how severely these should be pruned. Weak shoots should be pruned right back to two buds and stronger shoots back to five buds. Very few people ever prune newly planted roses hard enough

Fig. 4.4 (a & b). The pruning of a newly planted rose bush

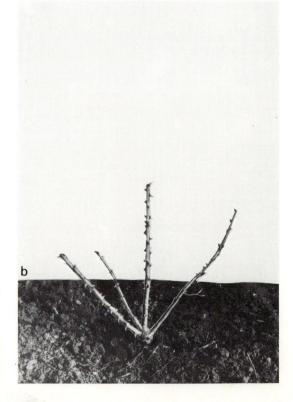

Initial pruning

Bedding roses planted late in the season are pruned at planting time. All roses can be pruned when planting but it is more usual with early plantings to allow them time to establish, pruning in March. All shoots are cut hard back: the weaker to two or three buds, the stronger to four or five (Figs. 4.3–4.4).

Standard hybrid teas and floribundas are pruned less severely to seven or eight buds of the union.

Climbing hybrid teas and floribundas are reduced to about half their original length. Too hard pruning of this group can result in their reversion to the bush types of which they are but sports.

Wichuriana climbers are cut to within 23cm (9in) of the ground, and **weeping standards** to the same distance from the union.

Shrub and **species roses** are restricted to three main stems, the rest being removed completely. Those remaining are cut to about a third of their original length, all side shoots growing into the bush are removed and the rest cut to within two buds of the main stems (Fig. 4.5).

Pruning of established roses flowering on current season's growth

Roses fall into two groups for pruning purposes: those flowering on current wood and those producing flowers on growth of the previous year. The main sections within the first group are: hybrid teas, floribundas, polyanthas, grandiflora, hybrid perpetuals, hybrid musks, miniatures, china roses and the *rugosa* forms.

Time of pruning

The timing of the pruning of this group flowering on current wood has long been controversial, every month from October to May having been recommended. Late March and early April is still the most popular period because it is claimed that shoots resulting are more likely to escape late frosts. But already at this time sap is rising and growth has begun, so some of the plant's energy will have been wasted, and in some varieties stems bleed following late pruning. Shoots which develop after this pruning are strong and succulent and therefore very susceptible to severe damage should there happen to be any late frosts. By May, disease organisms are active and likely to invade such damaged tissue.

Autumn pruning has now been generally discontinued. In a mild autumn pruning can force bushes into growth which is killed in the winter. Pruning when the bushes are dormant is undoubtedly the best time, and this is either January or February—though in some years growth never seems to cease completely. If, following early pruning, buds do start into growth the shoots develop very slowly and are hard, acclimatizing themselves as they grow and so are better able to withstand damage from late frosts—although they can be damaged by earlier severe weather.

The gardener who has difficulty in making up his mind about when to prune should try bushes at different times and then decide for himself.

The tools required

A pair of secateurs is adequate for most of the wood, plus loppers for thick wood and a narrow-bladed saw for the thickest or for awkward spots where secateurs cannot be used. Strong leather gloves make the operation less painful.

It is most important to ensure that cutting blades on secateurs are sharp and correctly set, with anvils in good condition. Blunt or badly set secateurs result in tears and bruising which may be followed by die-back and/or disease infection.

Techniques and principles of pruning

Bedding roses can flower well and profusely if never pruned, but the framework becomes hard and woody and grows upward with each year. Eventually new growth diminishes, flowers are of poorer quality, the bush is cluttered with dead and dying wood, and disease becomes a problem. Light pruning has a somewhat similar result even if the upward development is slower and there is no clutter, but flowers, though numerous, will be of poor quality. Hard pruning produces a small bush, well supplied with young growth on which flowers are few but of the best quality.

As with all pruning, one first carries out the

Fig. 4.5. The pruning of shrub or species roses
(a) A newly planted unpruned rose, indicating where the cuts should be made

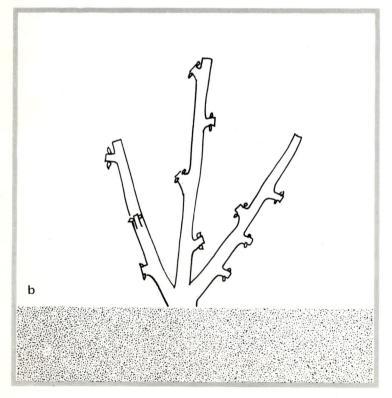

(b) Shows the rose pruned severely

Fig. 4.6. Bush rose prior to pruning showing wood of different ages. Three-year-old wood is represented by solid black; two-year-old wood is represented by lined shading; and one-year-old wood is represented unshaded

essentials: cutting out all dead and damaged wood and any that shows signs of disease, thinning out crowded branches and removing shoots growing into the centre of the bush. Look at the bush and observe the position, amount and ages of the wood. One-year-old wood is green, two-year-old is brownish-green and wood older than three years is brown or black (Fig. 4.6). From old wood will emerge shoots of one-year, two-year and even older wood, and there will always be a preponderance of older wood at the base of the bush. The aim should be to have a large percentage of one-year-old wood in the bush with most of this coming from, or near, ground-level.

Each year cut out some old wood, removing it to a point where young wood is breaking lower down, or cutting out completely any wood that has no younger wood, or very little, growing from it. At all times the aim should be to get rid of wood older than three years. On two-year-old wood, cut back to the lowest point at which young wood is developing, or if there is only terminal young growth, cut away about a third of the two-year wood. With one-year wood, cut back weak growth to two

or three buds and reduce the strong to a half or a third of its original length. Strong-growing varieties should be pruned less severely than weaker ones.

When pruning, make the cut just above the bud horizontally or slightly sloping outwards (Fig. 4.7). Cut always to an outward pointing bud. An exception is made on bushes growing on the outside of a bed when a shoot resulting from an outside bud would be damaged by the mower or perhaps tear the clothes of a passer-by. Stems in such a position can be cut so that the bud develops more or less parallel to the outer edge of the bed (Fig. 4.8).

Small pruning cuts heal readily but larger ones on three-year-old wood need to be sealed. Where a saw has been used, pare the cut surface with a knife before application. After winter pruning apply a spray combining both insecticide and fungicide to the bushes and the ground beneath.

Pruning removes wood in which food material is stored up and the plant has to make good the growth removed before it can flower. So whenever hard pruning is practised it must go along with applications of organic matter or

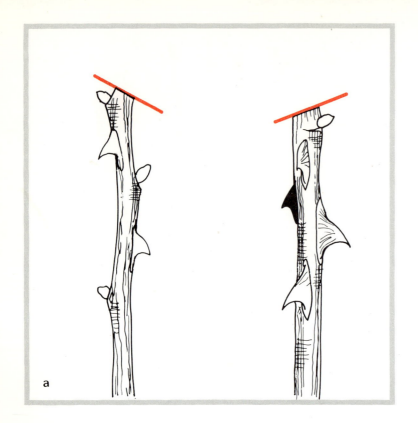

a

Fig. 4.7. Correct and incorrect pruning cuts
(a) Correct pruning cut. The cut should always be made so that it slopes slightly back and away from the bud at which it is made

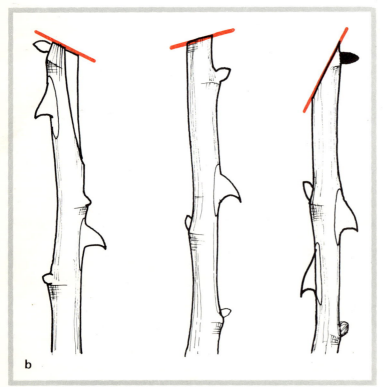

b

(b) Incorrect pruning cuts. The picture shows on the left the sort of cut made with a blunt instrument resulting in the tearing or crushing of the wood; the cut is also too close to the bud. The centre illustration shows a cut made too high leaving a snag of wood that will die, probably becoming infected and which could therefore kill the whole plant. The drawing on the right shows a cut made too close to the bud; this will result in the wood dying back to the bud below and present the same hazards as the cut made too high above the bud

Fig. 4.8. A plan view of a rose bush growing at the edge of a bed where pruning to an outward-pointing bud has to be modified so that resulting shoots do not overgrow the lawn. Cut to buds in red

a dressing of a general rose fertilizer. Beds of roses which have been regularly pruned and fertilized can still be in good healthy condition, flowering well and producing blooms of good quality after sixty years.

Following the January/February pruning, bushes grow away and by June are producing their first flush of flowers. After these have faded, the bushes need to be dead-headed. This improves their appearance and diverts energy which would be used up in the production of fruits into the production of more flowers. Dead-heading does not consist of just removing the dead head but of cutting down to where new growth is emerging, or removing about one-third of the new growth. This is in effect a type of summer pruning which leads on to a good second flush and, if repeated, to a third in some years.

Treatment of neglected roses

After reading so far you may have decided that something ought to be done about those roses which have never been pruned! Can they be brought back into order? Yes, it is possible to get them into good shape again, provided that the bushes are not too old. It cannot, however, be done in one year; you cannot correct long-standing neglect overnight.

Firstly remove all dead, damaged and diseased wood. Open up the centre of the bush, cutting out crossing branches and thinning where crowded; cut back all young wood to within two or three buds of their base. Feed well and apply a combined spray. This should stimulate the bushes into growth and some shoots should be produced low down on the bush.

In the following winter there must be more concentrated effort. Cut out all old wood arising above young shoots produced low down. Remove completely at least one old stem at, or as near as possible to, the ground. Reduce at least one of the older shoots by half and cut back hard all young shoots on the bush. Repeat the entire process the following year, cutting back all the time to where young growth is appearing low down on the bush. It will take at least three years to bring bushes back to normal but each year there should be an improvement in the amount of young wood produced and in the quality of flowers. If there is

a

Fig. 4.9. The pruning of a climbing rose (*a*) To be pruned properly, the whole rose needs to be taken away from the wall and laid out on the ground (*b*) where the unwanted wood can be cut out. When this has been done the remaining shoots, which will flower in the following summer, should be tied back to the wall (*c*)

no response after two years, the bushes are too old and should be removed.

Pruning of established roses flowering on one-year-old wood

Included in this group are climbing hybrid teas and floribundas, wichuriana climbers, weeping standards, most shrub roses and species. The best time for pruning these is immediately after flowering, but they are often left until the winter, especially when they have attractive fruits (Fig. 4.9).

Climbing hybrid teas and floribundas produce new growth from ground-level which should be tipped and tied in. The strongest varieties do this reasonably freely and so all wood which has flowered can be removed completely. Unfortunately most kinds do not refurnish readily and some, perhaps all, of their growth which has flowered has to be retained. Along these flowering canes, all the flowering laterals are cut hard back to two buds. The oldest shoots should always be removed whenever enough new shoots have been produced (Fig. 4.10).

Wichuriana climbers grow vigorously and produce an abundance of new shoots annually. All shoots, therefore, which have borne flowers are removed completely (Fig. 4.11). In fact so strong are some varieties that far more stems are produced than are required. Whenever enough shoots have been selected and tied in so as to be well spaced, the remainder should be removed; do not be tempted to keep all just because they are strong and healthy. If these are growing over a tree, however, they can be allowed to grow unpruned except for the removal of dead wood. When climbing over a pergola, old stems are allowed to keep growing to provide a good covering, but all laterals which have flowered are cut hard back. **Weeping standards** are just wichuriana climbers grafted on to a long

Fig. 4.10. Pruning of climbing
H.T. or floribunda roses

Fig. 4.11. Pruning of
Wichuriana climbers

stem. Following flowering, all stems which have borne flowers are removed completely.

Shrub and species roses can be left un-pruned, but without attention they become thickets of tangled growth, their centres choked with blind, dead or diseased twigs. Annual pruning is desirable to open up the centre of the bush and thin out crowded shoots. Tipping of young shoots in the winter months helps control mildew to which some kinds, eg *Rose × alba*, are particularly prone.

Roses with long arching branches can have them shortened. Some species, eg *R. spinosissima* (now properly *R. pimpinellifolia* though not widely known under that name), have a suckering habit and should have the oldest and weakest stems removed completely. One or two are grown for the winter effect of their stems, eg *R. omeiensis* var. *pteracantha* which has large red translucent thorns on its young stems; cut to ground-level in March just before new growth commences.

A few kinds are grown only for their coloured foliage, either summer, eg *R. rubrifolia*, or autumn, eg *R. virginiana*; these can be cut hard back in February to increase the size of their leaves. If, however, flowers and fruit are also wanted, cut back half of the shoots hard and tip the remainder.

Rose species which are tender are grown against a wall for protection. *R. banksiae* flowers on sub-laterals of the older wood and sometimes on wood produced the previous year; after training in a well-spaced framework, it does not need a great deal of pruning. Following flowering the surplus long shoots coming away from the wall are cut back, thinning takes place and the rest are tied in when some of the older wood is removed.

R. bracteata and its hybrid 'Mermaid' have pithy stems which are readily damaged by extreme cold, especially when wood fails to ripen properly after a wet summer. The young stems are very brittle and easily snapped off so care must be exercised when tying in. Carry out pruning in April, removing any winter-damaged wood, cutting back shoots which have flowered and thinning generally. When growing well, large amounts of shoots are produced and in a wet summer an end-of-August thinning of non-flowering shoots will aid the ripening of wood.

Special types of pruning

Hedges

Some of the more vigorous bushy kinds of roses can be used to make low hedges up to about 1·8m (6ft) in height. These are informal, producing flowers, and so are trimmed rather than clipped to strict formality. Amongst suitable floribundas are the old variety 'Frensham' or the newer 'Queen Elizabeth'; many shrub roses make good hedges, eg the hybrid musks and 'Nevada'; and of the many species suitable are *R. rugosa* and its hybrids and *R. rubiginosa* and its hybrid group, the 'Penzance Briars'.

Plant in well-prepared ground at 90–120cm (3–4ft) intervals and cut hard back to about 23cm (9in) to produce strong growth from ground-level. In the following winter, remove about half of the new wood, and so on each year until the hedge has reached its maximum height. Hedges flowering on current season's growth are trimmed to shape in February and any dead wood removed. When flowers are from the previous year's growth trim after flowering.

Tie-down roses

This is a method of training strong-growing roses to induce maximum flowering. Some of these strong growers produce up to 1·8m (6ft) of growth in one growing season with flowers on the ends of these long stems. During the last century, when hybrid perpetuals were the only roses which flowered more than once, their vigour was a problem and the tie-down system was devised to increase flowering. Today only a few of this group are grown, eg 'Hugh Dickson', but this method is well suited to such strong growers as 'Zephryn Drouhin', 'Frau Karl Drushki', 'Uncle Walter', some of the hybrid musks as well as 'Guinea' and 'High Noon'.

During the spring the sap, as we all know, rises to the highest part of the stem and the apical bud extends. When a bush is pruned, the top two or three buds develop and continue to extend, their ultimate length being governed by food material available and weather conditions. But if the shoot is tied down so that it is horizontal, all buds on the shoot are at the same height, so all develop equally. The tying down is done on a metal or wooden framework

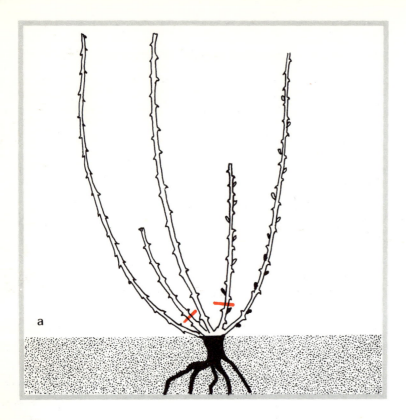

a

Fig. 4.12. Tie-down roses. The training of tie-down roses showing
(a) a young plant being pruned in its second winter after planting in preparation for tying down to a metal frame

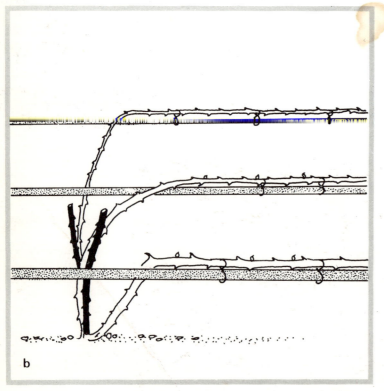

b

(b) the pruning of an established tie-down rose when the oldest flowering shoots are cut away

Pruning a standard rose. It is worth noticing that in addition to shortening back the shoots, weak shoots should be removed altogether.

Rosa 'China Town' trained as a tie-down rose. The main shoots are bent over and secured to the framework of wires.

Above: Using loppers to remove shoots from a rose that would be too tough for secateurs. More secateurs are ruined by attempting to use them to cut wood that is too thick or too tough for them than by any other type of misuse.

Pruning a peach. The sequence shows the reduction in the number of shoots. The final picture shows the end result, a fine crop of peaches.

Fig. 4.12. (c) The training of tie-down roses: on young ones, cut back the short shoots on which flowers were produced in the preceding summer

(appropriate to the size of the bed) which is fixed at 45cm (18in) above ground-level. Its design is immaterial; it can be latticed, of concentric circles or shaped like wheel spokes.

Following a well-spaced planting, the stems are cut hard back to about five buds; weak shoots are cut even harder. In the following season several very strong shoots will develop. At pruning time these are tipped and tied to the framework so as to be horizontal, all of the stem remaining at one level. During the follow-ing summer short lateral growth will develop from each bud on the tied-down stem and produce flowers. In the winter months these laterals are cut back to two buds and any strong new growth is tied in. As the allotted space is filled, some of the oldest shoots can be removed each year (Fig. 4.12).

Pruning should be carried out in January or February, but as there is so much tying which cannot be carried out in gloves December pruning is more comfortable.

5 Tools and Equipment

Tools used for pruning are numerous and varied and each has been devised for a specific purpose. There are three groups: knives, secateurs and saws (but *see also* Chapter 13 for hedge trimming tools).

Knives

Today the use of knives is limited because few people know how to use them properly, but in

Fig. 5.1. A pruning knife. There is a definite art to using these knives and any competent rose nurseryman will demonstrate it to you. If you can master the art it will give a good, clean cut

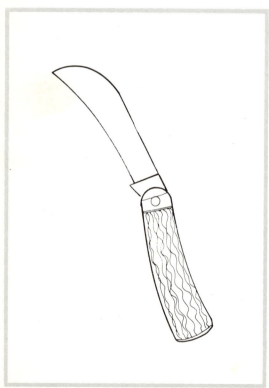

the hands of a skilled operator they are still the best pruning tool (Fig. 5.1). There are a number on the market, of differing sizes and patterns, which are sold as pruning knives, but in fact almost any kind of knife can be used for pruning provided the blade is of good steel, capable of keeping a good edge, and is firmly set into the handle so that it cannot come loose under pressure.

A pruning knife must be sharp; a blunt knife is useless and can also be dangerous. More wounds are inflicted with blunt knives than with sharp ones, because more pressure has to be applied to make them cut and this is when they are likely to slip. When pruning, hold the branch below the point where the cut is to be made. Start with the knife behind the branch, just below the level of the chosen bud. With a slightly upward movement make the cut at an angle, to finish just above the bud.

A knife should be sharpened on an oil-stone. Inspection of the blade will indicate how it was sharpened in the factory: often one side of the blade is flat and the other has been sharpened at an angle; sometimes both have been sharpened at an angle. Where possible, sharpen to the same angle as previously. However, some people find it difficult to keep a knife blade at a fixed angle, and they may have to compromise and sharpen both sides flat on the stone.

Keep your pruning knife for just this task. Don't use it for cutting any old thing or for prising tacks out of wood or the edge of the blade will soon become chipped—even with constant care this can too easily happen. If the blade does become chipped, grind the edge down until it is again straight and then sharpen in the normal manner. Once a blade has been sharpened a keen edge can be produced and maintained as necessary by use of a carborundum stone.

Though knives may not be in regular use for pruning there are some jobs for which they have to be used: paring smooth the rind after sawing off a branch; gouging out diseased material from a branch prior to painting with a wound protectant; trimming back young growth that has been damaged by late frosts; and removing twiggy growths along trunks so as not to leave basal buds. After use the blade should always be wiped clean and any matter adhering removed by emery paper. Rub the blade with an oily cloth and put a drop of oil on the pivot to make for easier movement.

Secateurs

Secateurs carry out the work that was formerly done with the pruning knife. Their use requires little effort and no special skill; they are an indispensable aid to the gardener. There are two main types: the parrot-beak with two cutting blades, and the anvil with one (Figs. 5.2 & 5.3).

Parrot-beak type

These are so called because of the shape of the cutting blades. They are available in several sizes, the products of different manufacturers varying slightly in design and size range. One type has a swivel handle which takes wrist fatigue out of the job. These are used in one hand and are capable of cutting stems of up to half an inch easily and up to three-quarters of an inch with care. Do not try to cut heavier wood with them. When cutting use a straight action and avoid twisting the blades.

After use, remove ingrained dirt with emery paper and before putting away wipe all parts with an oily cloth and put a spot of oil on the pivot and spring. When not actually working with them keep the catch on and the blades together. Most manufacturers or their agents will service their secateurs for a small fee, and if these are in regular use annual attention is desirable.

Fig. 5.2. (a) Parrot-beak secateurs   (b) In action

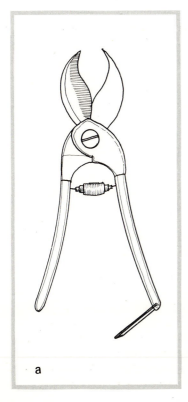

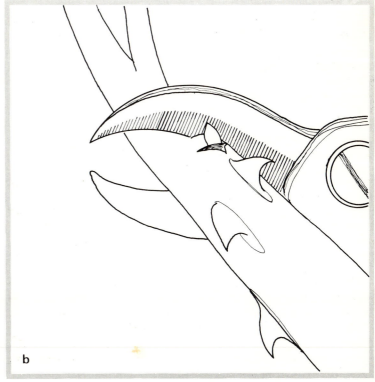

a

b

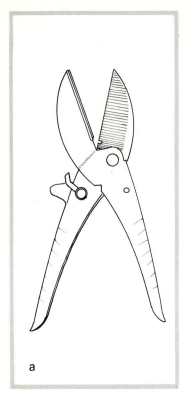

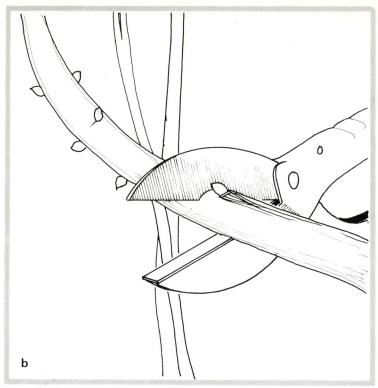

Fig. 5.3. (a) Anvil-type secateurs   (b) In action; the cut should be made with the blade on top of the bud so that the actual position of the cut can be seen

Anvil type

These secateurs have an anvil which holds the stem while the single blade does the cutting. They are available in several sizes and with one or two special modifications, eg for cutting wire. They need a little more attention in handling than the previous type. Make the blade do the cutting; do not try to make the anvil push the stem against the cutting edge. Always have the blade where it can be seen and place the blade above the bud when making the cut. Again, do not attempt to cut wood that is too thick; like the parrot-beak type, these will easily cope with wood up to half an inch, and with care up to three-quarters. Avoid twisting the secateurs when cutting as this strains them and causes the blade to cut off centre, which results in bruising or tearing of the bark. The blade must be sharp at all times and the anvil in good condition. After continued use the blade can cause a groove along the anvil or ingrained dirt may accumulate to provide an uneven surface and inefficient cutting with bruising and tearing will certainly follow. Sending your secateurs away annually for service ensures that they remain in good condition.

When a pruning job is finished see that all ingrained dirt, either on the blade or the anvil, is removed with emery paper and all metal parts are rubbed with an oily cloth. A drop of oil should be introduced into the pivot. Fasten when not in use so that the blade is kept against the anvil.

Long-handled secateurs or loppers

These are modifications of the anvil or parrot-beak type on handles about 45cm (18in) long. The blade or blades open wider, and as with the longer handles there is more leverage the loppers can cope easily with wood up to three-quarters of an inch and with care up to one inch; their longer handles give a greater reach. Two hands are needed to operate them (Fig. 5.4).

Long-arms or long-armed pruners

These are anvil-type secateurs fixed on the end of a pole which comes in varying lengths up

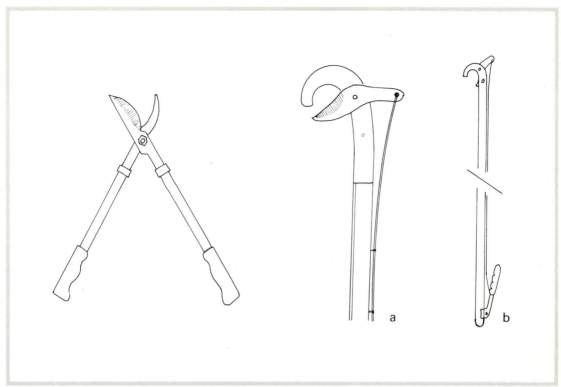

Fig. 5.4. Long-handled pruners, also known as stumpers or loppers. The extra length of the handles gives one greater leverage and these are designed to be used on thick and old wood

Fig. 5.5 (a & b). Long-arm pruners. These are useful for removing high branches from trees.

to 2·7m (9ft). The single cutting blade is operated by a wire attached to a handle. When the handle is in the up position the blade is open; to operate, pull down the handle and this drives the blade on to its anvil. This high-reaching tool also needs two hands, one to hold and one to operate (Fig. 5.5a & b).

Saws

Joiners' or carpenters' saws can be used for pruning, but saws manufactured for the job are to be preferred for they stand up better to the rougher work and are easier to insert and use in difficult places. Saws take over from secateurs when branches of more than one inch thickness have to be cut.

Narrow-bladed saw

This type has one cutting edge, is between half an inch and an inch in width, and has a folding handle (Fig. 5.6a & b). It can deal with wood up to one and a half inches in diameter but above this the work becomes tiring. Its main

use is to saw awkwardly placed small branches or to remove one branch where several are growing close together and loppers cannot be used.

Pruning saw

This is two-edged, with larger teeth on one side than on the other (Fig. 5.7). It is used for branches up to perhaps 8cm (3in) in diameter, the initial rougher work being carried out with the larger teeth and the final finishing cut made with the smaller. The one trouble with this type of saw is that it is unsuitable for dealing with branches growing close together, as damage can be caused by the second cutting edge. After use, as with all saws, remove saw-dust from the teeth with a wire brush and wipe with an oily rag. Send away regularly for sharpening.

Grecian saw

The curved blade has teeth along one side only (Fig. 5.8). It can be used for the same tasks as the pruning saw and is preferable to it.

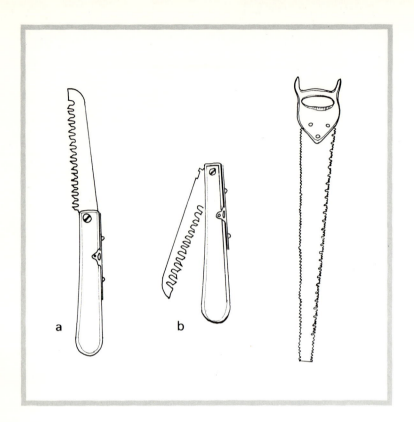

Fig. 5.6(a & b). Narrow-bladed pruning saw. This folding type is particularly useful

Fig. 5.7. Pruning saw. Note that the teeth on one side of the blade are much coarser than the teeth on the other side. It is thus a dual-purpose tool

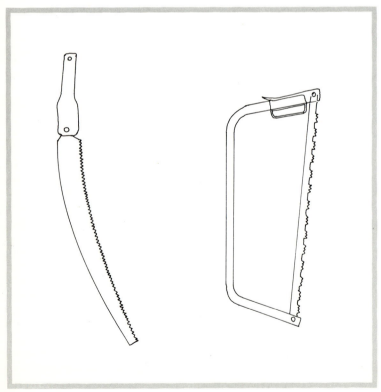

Fig. 5.8. Grecian saw. This is useful for cutting old wood in confined spaces

Fig. 5.9. Bow saw. This is normally used for removing large branches

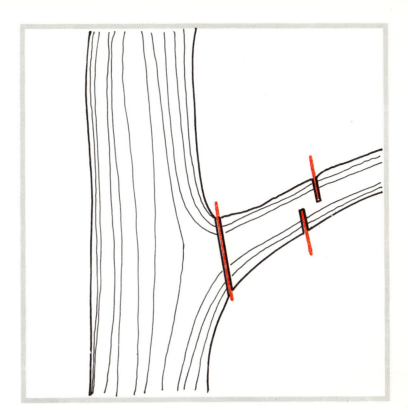

Fig. 5.10. Removal of a large branch. The sequence of cutting is: 1 undercut; 2 saw down until branch breaks away between cuts 1 & 2; 3 remove remaining stub

Bow saw

Here we have a metal frame with a detachable saw blade which is capable of dealing with all branches as long as there is enough space to operate; replace with a new blade when the old one shows signs of wear (Fig. 5.9).

Taking off a branch

When sawing off a small branch, take its weight so that it does not break away and tear the bark. If one does not have a free hand or if the branch is large, it should first be undercut until the wood begins to pinch; then remove the saw and start on the top of the branch. Don't worry about being directly above the lower cut. This does not matter. As the branch parts from the tree it will break cleanly between the two cuts. The stub remaining should then be cut off neatly, finishing just slightly proud of the trunk (Fig. 5.10).

A large limb should be removed in pieces. When in the centre of the tree or high in the crown, large branches or parts to be cut away should be roped to higher branches so they do not fall and damage wood below (pp. 141–3).

Ladders and steps

When pruning has to be carried out on trees and even on some large shrubs, some if not all of the branches may be out of reach and a ladder or steps will be necessary.

Steps should be in good condition and securely placed. When working on soft soil stand the legs on wooden planks. Household steps can be used but are not very comfortable for prolonged use. Aluminium platform steps are best, being light and durable with a relatively large area from which to work.

Ladders for tree work again should be in good condition and firmly placed both at the top and the bottom. Never work on a path without having someone below to hold the ladder, and in windy weather, tie the top securely before beginning. A safety belt gives a feeling of security and leaves both hands free. Try to work above the branch you are removing as this is less tiring than having to reach upwards and saw from beneath. And when dropping branches have a care for persons or property underneath. You may be legally responsible for any injury done. Finally, after having removed

55

the wood, clear up, burn the twiggy growth and saw up into lengths the stout branches.

Sealing applications

The removal of any part of a plant causes a wound which has to heal. Just below the bark of a shrub or tree is a single, continuous layer of cells known as the cambium. Following a cut, these cells begin to divide, producing callus tissue which forms in a ring around the circumference of the cut and continues to increase inwards for varying distances, depending on the size of cut, age, vigour, condition and kind of tree or shrub. On small young branches, the entire end of the cut may be sealed in this way, but on thicker and older wood healing may not be complete and callus may only form around the edge of the cut.

Roughly cut, broken, torn or bruised wood is slow to heal because the ring of cambium has been broken and a complete seal is rarely possible. Broken branches or those roughly cut with a large toothed saw, should have the stubs taken off with a finer toothed saw and the edge of the bark pared smooth with a sharp knife. Where tears have taken place, all the edges of exposed bark should be pared smooth.

The importance of sealing

Fungus diseases are spread by spores which float about in the air. They can enter a plant through a wound and as soon as they take hold they multiply rapidly. There are two types of disease: parasitic, infecting living tissue, and saprophytic, invading dead tissue.

Parasitic diseases such as silver leaf spread throughout the plant along the conducting tissue, causing death of the branches as they proceed. They will always have advanced beyond the wood where external symptoms appear, and to cut back to healthy tissue all wood showing interior brown staining has to be removed. Saprophytic diseases attack the central part or heart wood of the tree, which consists of dead tissue—only the outer sheath is living. The spread of these diseases can cause cavities, and if continuous can invade the trunk, so weakening the tree. Some saprophytic diseases can also become parasitic; coral spot is one such disease.

The formation of callus tissue prevents the entry of disease organisms and so it is important that this healing process should be as rapid as possible. It is quite fast on young shoots but it can take a long time where old and large branches have been removed. All cuts above an inch should be treated with a wound dressing which provides a protection against disease entry until the healing process is complete. There are a number of proprietary makes available.

For those trees that are slow to heal, especially in the winter months (eg magnolias), pruning may be more suitably done in the late summer when callus tissue forms more quickly.

6 Pruning Control of Pests and Diseases

Pests

Aphids
PLANTS ATTACKED Very many.

SYMPTOMS Colonies under leaves or on growing points. Distortion of leaves and growing points followed by early defoliation or death of growing point. Aphids spread virus diseases.

CONTROL Cut out badly infested shoots and burn; spray with malathion or lindane.

Leaf miners
PLANTS ATTACKED Various members of Compositae and *Ilex* species and cultivars.

SYMPTOMS Tunnels or blotches within the leaves, at first white but becoming brown as the leaf ages.

CONTROL In light attacks spray with malathion: this should kill the pest though the damage will remain; in bad attacks cut away unsightly growth. When attacks are frequent, spray annually with lindane as the young growth begins to develop.

Stem borers
PLANTS ATTACKED Various, particularly pines.

SYMPTOMS Dying of young shoots, often the leader.

CONTROL Cut out and burn infested shoots.

Woolly aphids
PLANTS ATTACKED Apples, ornamental crab apples.

SYMPTOMS Colonies of pests surrounded by a cotton-wool-like mass. In bad attacks swollen, gall-like growth appears on branches.

CONTROL During pruning cut out infested shoots; spray with malathion.

Diseases

Black spot
PLANTS ATTACKED Roses.

SYMPTOMS Black blotches on leaves (Fig. 6.1).

CONTROL Gather up and burn fallen leaves and prunings; spray with captan or benomyl.

Brown rot
PLANTS ATTACKED Apples and pears, both edible and ornamental.

SYMPTOMS Brown soft rot of fruit on which appear grey or buff coloured pustules; during the winter the infected mummified fruits remain hanging on the trees. Spores can spread from these and infect buds of spurs and twigs, resulting in die-back.

CONTROL Remove all mummified fruit and burn; spray with captan.

Bud blast
PLANTS ATTACKED Rhododendrons, particularly garden hybrids.

SYMPTOMS Dead flower buds covered with dark grey fungal growths.

CONTROL Hand-pick and burn infected buds. This disease is spread by the rhododendron

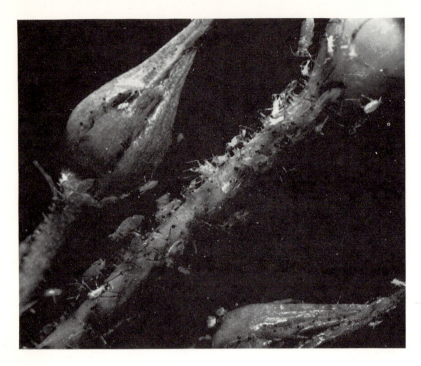

Fig. 6.1. Aphids: a ubiquitous pest whose numbers can often be controlled by spraying

leaf hopper and these pests should be controlled by spraying, following flowering, with lindane or malathion to which is added zineb to control disease spores.

Canker
PLANTS ATTACKED Various, particularly apples and pears, ornamental as well as edible.

SYMPTOMS Dead areas on branches with raised, gnarled edges surrounding dead, papery, often peeling bark.

CONTROL Most common on old trees or those in poor condition—a disease of neglect. Cut out branches where infections occur and burn. Where this is not possible, gouge out infected material with a sharp knife or chisel; paint all cuts with a wound protectant.

Coral spot
PLANTS ATTACKED Various, particularly *Acer*.

SYMPTOMS Orange pustules on infected wood.

CONTROL This disease attacks dead wood

from which it may spread to living, especially when this is in poor health. In some plants it will spread from dead wood to healthy material causing die-back of branches and in bad attacks the entire tree may die. Cut out all dead and diseased wood and burn; seal all cut surfaces. In bad attacks or with susceptible plants such as *Acer*, spray with zineb.

Die-back/grey mould botrytis
PLANTS ATTACKED Various, but particularly roses.

SYMPTOMS In winter it can be recognized on dead twigs by a water-stained appearance of the bark. In summer the die-back is accompanied by grey mould.

CONTROL Cut out infected material and burn; follow by spraying with captan.

Dutch elm
PLANTS ATTACKED All kinds of elm.

SYMPTOMS The disease is spread by the elm beetle whose galleries can be seen under the bark on infected branches. Dead wood in crown of tree; early yellowing and defoliation of infected branches.

CONTROL Where infection is light, cut out and burn diseased wood; in severe cases, fell and burn.

Fireblight
PLANTS ATTACKED Most genera in the Rosaceae, the following being particularly susceptible, *Cotoneaster*, *Crataegus*, *Pyracantha*, *Pyrus* and *Sorbus*.

SYMPTOMS Dead twigs with blackened dead leaves still hanging, looking as though burnt; seen in June and July.

CONTROL Cut out and burn infected shoots. After each cut, dip cutting implement in methylated spirit to prevent spreading disease agent; seal all wounds.

Poplar canker
PLANTS ATTACKED Most poplar species.

SYMPTOMS Long narrow patches with sunken bark and gumming.

CONTROL If the disease is extensive, no control is possible; fell and burn. In light infections cut out or gouge out infected wood back to healthy wood and seal all wounds; sterilize all cutting implements.

Powdery mildew
PLANTS ATTACKED Many.

SYMPTOMS White mildew on young leaves and stem.

CONTROL Cut out and burn infected shoot tips; spray with karathane after pruning and at intervals of 7–10 days during the summer.

Silver leaf
PLANTS ATTACKED Various, but particularly peaches, cherries, apples and plums, both eating and ornamental.

SYMPTOMS Leaves take on a silvery or leaden appearance and die-back follows.

CONTROL Prior to mid-July cut all infected material back to healthy wood; seal all cuts. Burn infected material.

7 Alphabetical List of Genera

Abbreviations

D	Deciduous	S	Shrub
E	Evergreen	T	Tree
L	Leafless	C	Conifer
		CL	Climber

ABELIA D S Most species are tender and need a sheltered position or wall. In late April, remove winter damage, thin crowded shoots and remove some old wood.

ABELIOPHYLLUM D S A shrub with a sprawling habit, usually grown against a wall to give protection to its early flowers. After flowering, cut out shoots on which flowers have been produced. If grown as a free-standing shrub, rather harder pruning is necessary following flowering to correct the sprawling habit.

ABIES (fir) E C Select a single leader and retain all side branches.

ABUTILON D S All species are tender and usually grown as wall shrubs. In May cut out

Fig. 7.1. *Abutilon megapotamicum*

winter damage and thin out crowded shoots. *Abutilon vitifolium* should be treated as a free-standing shrub and succeeds best where there is some summer humidity; the only pruning needed is dead-heading (Fig. 7.1). *A. × Suntense* is a new and spectacular hardy hybrid which tends to blow over unless fairly hard pruning follows flowering, in early June.

ACACIA E S/T
All species are tender and require the protection of a south wall. Ensure that the base of the wall is well clothed and kept covered right throughout training; as most species are trees in their natural form growth is upwards and flowers too often are out of sight. Established pruning consists of dead-heading, thinning and the removal of dead wood in spring or early summer.

ACER (maple) D S/T
A large family of varying habits, size and attractions all of which have to be considered when pruning.

Trees are trained to a central leader which is feathered. If the leader is lost a new one must be trained in or the opposite buds will produce two leaders; in some species it is difficult to retain a leader. Carry out pruning when fully dormant: some species bleed if cut when the sap is rising. Bushes may be allowed to have several leaders though often a central one is trained in but with all side shoots retained.

Coloured leaf forms of *A. negundo* should never be pruned hard otherwise the resulting shoots revert to green. Training in the early days should consist of little more than pinching. Those trees grown for their bark should, through feathering, have their trunks exposed as soon as possible; an annual trimming of the previous year's growth on the snake bark maples will result in long colourful young stems. All species are likely to suffer damage from the fungus known as coral spot. This initially infects dead wood but spreads to the living, killing stems and even branches; if it girdles a young tree death can result.

ACTINIDIA D CL
Slightly tender, vigorous twiners that need plenty of space. Once a well-spaced framework has been achieved by training in several long stems opposite and parallel, young stems are cut back in April to within two or three buds of this framework;

repeat the process in July so as to build up a spur system.

AESCULUS (horse chestnut) D S/T
Often these trees are slow growing in their early years. Select a leader and feather; retrain a new leader if the original is lost, or two will result because of opposite buds. There is a tendency to produce strong shoots low down on the tree and these should be removed, preferably during the winter months. With age the lower branches droop and touch the ground, so in training do not allow the lowest branches to develop under 3·6m (12ft). *A. parviflora* does not form a tree but clumps of vertical stems. Occasionally cut out the oldest of these and restrict spread if the clumps become invasive. This work should be done during the winter.

AILANTHUS (tree of heaven) D T
Makes very strong growth when young: 2·7m (9ft) in one year is not unknown. Shoots are pithy and subject to winter damage, especially if not properly ripened. Keep to a single leader, retraining if the original is lost.

The strong young shoots with their very large compound leaves are sometimes used to give sub-tropical effects in gardens. To achieve this, cut all shoots back to ground-level in spring, just as the buds begin to swell, and feed copiously (Fig. 7.2). Take care not to damage the root system otherwise extensive suckering will result.

AKEBIA D CL
Strong climbers which need plenty of space and which will become an unmanageable tangle unless regular pruning is practised. In June cut out all shoots which have flowered and thin drastically any remaining. If pruning has been neglected, shear off at about 90cm (3ft) from the ground, retrain a framework and start again.

ALNUS (alder) D S/T
Plants for damp soils, grown especially for their winter catkins. Often they are allowed to develop without special training except for thinning out crowded branches. If a tree is required, select a central leader and feather. Coloured leaf forms should be moderately hard pruned after flowering.

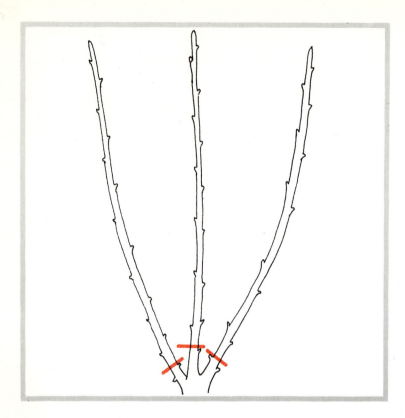

Fig. 7.2. Coppicing or hard pruning, to achieve a subtropical foliage effect. This type of pruning is only suitable for one or two trees such as *Ailanthus glandulosa* or *Paulownia tomentosa*. The former when treated this way in rich soil will produce leaves up to 90cm (3ft) in length

AMELANCHIER (snowy mespilus)

D S/T For pruning purposes, there are two types: one suckers and remains a shrub, the other becomes tree-like. The first is pruned in January when the oldest stems are removed; for the second, a central leader is trained, all side shoots being reduced but retained as long as possible.

AMPELOPSIS

D CL All are strong growers which support themselves by tendrils and need plenty of space. They are well suited for growing through a tree where no pruning is required. If space is restricted train in a number of rods (mature shoots) and in January cut back all young shoots to within two or three buds of the rods. Bleeding will follow if pruning is delayed until the sap begins to rise.

ARALIA

D S Stems arising from a root-stock are stout and pithy and liable to be damaged in winter if they do not ripen properly. The chief attraction is the large compound leaves of which there are variegated forms. Retain only a few stems and remove the rest at ground-level each spring.

ARAUCARIA (monkey puzzle)

D C *A. araucana* is the only species which is hardy in the British Isles. It makes a large tree and needs plenty of space. Select a central leader and retain all side branches until they die naturally.

ARBUTUS

E S/T Some species are tender. Shrubs require little attention except to thin growths in April. Trees should have a central leader with all side shoots reduced but retained as long as possible. *A. menziesii, andrachne* and × *andrachnoides* have attractive barks; trunks can be exposed early by feathering.

ARCTOSTAPHYLOS

E S/T Some species are tender. Prostrate forms may need thinning otherwise stems will grow over each other, shutting out light and causing the leaves to die off. The tree forms are usually trained to three or more leaders which are feathered during April to expose their colourful trunks.

ARISTOLOCHIA

D CL Only one or two species are hardy in Britain and they need

62

a warm wall. These are vigorous growers requiring plenty of space. After flowering drastically thin out shoots and reduce those that are wandering.

ARONIA (chokéberry) D S If grown for flowers and fruit as well as autumn colour, thin out only the crowded branches during winter. If grown only for autumn colour, reduce all shoots by half.

ARTEMISIA E S A few species are woody and these are somewhat tender. Remove winter damage in May and trim to shape. As these plants are grown for their foliage, flower spikes can be removed as they form.

ATRIPLEX E S Some species are tender. All kinds tend to sprawl, especially if grown in shade or a rich soil. Trim moderately hard in April to correct this habit.

AUCUBA E S Trim to shape in April occasionally cutting out some of the oldest wood. This shrub will respond to hard pruning if it becomes too large.

AZALEA *see* **Rhododendron**

AZARA E S/T All species are tender and, except in the mildest parts of the country, need the protection of a wall where they are fan trained. *A. microphylla* is the hardiest species and can make a free-standing shrub or even a small tree in favoured districts. After flowering remove shoots which have carried flowers, remove winter damage and carry out some thinning.

BALLOTA E S Slightly tender sprawling shrubs grown for their foliage. Prune hard in April to keep tidy and again in midsummer if growth becomes rampant.

BAMBOOS E S (The different genera are all included under this heading for their pruning is identical.) Cut out discoloured, dead and thin stems, as well as those which have flowered in April. The bamboos which spread by underground runner can be invasive and some means of confining them may be necessary. Once flowering begins death fol-

lows, not always immediately but each year thereafter the clumps decline.

BERBERIS D/E S Some evergreen kinds are tender and need shelter. All evergreen berberis species should be pruned after flowering, but if berries are wanted delay until the following April when those shoots having borne fruit are removed. Most deciduous kinds form dense thickets and these should be thinned in July, removing completely at ground-level. If old bushes become unmanageable they can be cut down to ground-level after flowering for they will readily break away again.

BETULA (birch) D T All birches have attractive barks even though these do not develop until the trees are several years old. Select a central leader and feather, exposing the trunk eventually to about 3m (10ft) before allowing branches to form. The leader in birches is frequently lost, and as leader competition is common reduce multiple leaders. Any pruning of birches should be carried out when fully dormant for bleeding will occur following cutting when the sap is rising.

One or two species such as *B. populifolia* naturally develop several trunks, which can be an interesting feature in a landscape. To produce several trunks in a birch, cut the sapling back at planting time to about 90cm (3ft), select the strongest shoots and train each as a separate leader.

Weeping birches should have a central leader trained to a support until there is a clear stem of 3·6m (12ft).

BUDDLEIA D/E S Many species are tender and need a south or west wall for protection; these are trained fan-wise, ensuring that the lowest part of the wall is kept clothed.

Buddleias which flower on current season's growth, eg *B. davidii*, are cut hard back to a framework in the winter; tender species are similarly treated in April. Buddleias which flower on the previous year's growth, eg *B. globosa*, are pruned following flowering when the shoots which have carried flowers are removed.

Buddleia alternifolia is best treated as a standard. Select the strongest shoot, removing the others, and tie to a stake; continue feathering until there is a clear stem of at least 1·2m (4ft) after which natural development can be allowed.

BUXUS (box) E S/T If of tree form, select a single leader, removing competition; side shoots are reduced but retained as long as possible except if too crowded. The bush kinds, of which there are many different forms, should be trimmed to shape in April when some corrective pruning may be necessary, especially if heavy snow has caused any damage.

CALLICARPA D S All species are tender to some degree. Prune in April cutting out any winter damage and thinning out crowded shoots.

CALLISTEMON (bottle brush) E S All species are tender and need the protection of a south wall. Growth is continuous, flowers being produced just behind the growing point. Seed capsules can remain on the shrub for years but, if left, these gradually reduce the rate of growth producing a gaunt,

rather untidy bush. Prune then after flowering, removing the spent flowers and trim to shape (Fig. 7.3).

CALLUNA (ling) E S Trim over the clumps in March, removing old flowers and most of last year's growth. The dwarf forms such as 'Foxii' and 'Foxii Nana' are not pruned at all except to remove dead wood. Plants grown just for foliage are often best trimmed as the flower spikes form for the colours of flower and foliage often clash.

CALOCEDRUS E C No pruning should be necessary once a single leader has been trained.

CALYCANTHUS D S Remove some of the oldest wood and thin during April.

CAMELLIA E S Some species are tender and need wall protection. *C. japonica* and its many forms are hardy though often flowerbud tender. Dead-heading is desirable on those

Fig. 7.3. *Callistemon* or bottle brush

Fig. 7.4. *Camellia*

kinds which do not shed their spent flowers; at the same time trim to shape or to restrict growth (Fig. 7.4).

Camellia japonica sports freely and several colours can appear amongst flowers on one bush. Branches bearing different coloured flowers should be traced to their source and removed. *C. sasanqua* and *C. cuspidata* are autumn-flowering species and if pruning is necessary carry this out in April.

Tender species and some of the forms of *C. japonica* may be grown as wall shrubs. Fan train a well-spaced framework and allow side branches to develop just sufficiently to fill the intervening spaces; remove surplus shoots as well as any coming away from the wall.

CAMPSIS D CL These slightly tender climbers need full sun and a south wall. They are strong growers, attaching themselves to supports by climbing roots. Once a well-shaped framework has been trained with the lower part of the wall well-clothed, all side shoots should be cut back in early spring to within two or three buds.

CARPINUS (hornbeam) D T Train to a single leader, feathering until the required length of stem has been produced. Carry out pruning when fully dormant, for if delayed until the sap starts to rise bleeding will follow. Coral spot can be a troublesome disease both on dead and living wood.

CARYOPTERIS D S Unless the wood is thoroughly ripened, die-back is common. In April cut back all young shoots to a framework which is best trained on a short leg.

CASTANEA (sweet chestnut) D T This tree produces the edible nuts but in many parts of Britain it is rare for nuts to reach sufficient size. In the garden it is sometimes grown as a specimen tree for its deeply furrowed bark is pleasing. Select a central leader and feather until a sufficient length of trunk has been achieved. With age, wood becomes brittle and trees shed large limbs. The spread, therefore, of mature limbs is best reduced by periodically shortening large branches.

CATALPA (Indian bean tree) D S/T
Most often trained as a large shrub with
several leaders; when established, keep the
centre of the bush open. All species form small
trees and if desired as such should have a single
leader, with side branches reduced and gradually removed. Pruning, when necessary, is
carried out in March or April when the old seed
pods are removed. When grown for their
coloured foliage pruning should be moderately
hard.

CEANOTHUS D/E S All evergreens are
tender and the deciduous kinds reasonably
hardy.

The evergreen kinds can be, and are often,
grown against a wall. Plant from containers and
ensure that plants are not root-bound. It is
usual to train a parallel framework to cover the
wall, ensuring as always that the lower parts
are kept clothed. Prune after flowering, cutting
only the young growth hard back to the framework. If treated as free-standing shrubs, they
are trained to several leaders and trimmed each
year, following flowering, back to this framework; winter damage is removed and some
thinning may be desirable. Avoid cutting into
old wood as this is slow to break.

The deciduous kinds flower on current season's growth which is cut down to ground-level
or to a framework in April.

CEDRUS (cedar) E C Young trees are
triangular in outline but with age all develop
flat tops. Training of cedars is often neglected
as the many badly-shaped trees about the
countryside witness. Select and retain a central
leader, removing any competition, multiple
leaders, or strong growth that develops from
low down.

CELASTRUS D CL These are strong
climbers best suited to growing over trees
where they can be left to their own devices. If
space is restricted, annual thinning is necessary
to keep them within bounds; this is best carried
out in July when it is easier to recognize dead
wood.

CEPHALOTAXUS E C Some kinds
tend to sprawl and rather drastic pruning in
April may be necessary to correct this.

CERATOSTIGMA E S All species are
somewhat tender, but though they may be cut
back to ground-level in a cold winter they usually break away freely so long as the roots are
undamaged. Flowering is on current season's
growth and all growth surviving the winter is
cut back to ground-level in April.

CERCIDIPHYLLUM D S/T In the
wild this makes a large tree sometimes with
several trunks. Ideally a single leader should
be selected, the side shoots being reduced and
gradually removed. If a multi-stemmed trunk
is required, head the sapling back to 90cm (3ft)
at planting and select the strongest three
shoots, training each as you would a single
leader. More often this is treated as a shrub in
gardens and trained to a single leader with all
side shoots retained. Some thinning may be
desirable and, if space is limited, trimming
back of young growth in March.

CERCIS (Judas tree) D T It is not easy
to train and retain a single leader but this is
the best method. Reduce side shoots and
gradually remove them. *Cercis* is generally
grown as a shrub, with little pruning. It is,
however, important to train in a satisfactory
framework and give a light trimming after
flowering to remove the immature seed pods.
The production of these can be excessive and
if left will reduce vigour and extension growth.

CHAENOMELES **(Japanese
quince)** D S These are spur-bearing shrubs
and once regular flowering begins, little pruning is required. Select several leaders and train
to a well-balanced framework. An encourage-
ment to help in producing spurs in early years
is to cut back all side shoots to three or four
buds in the winter months. It is important to
keep the centre of the bush open and any shoots
intruding should be removed.

If grown as wall shrubs to gain some protection for the precocious flowers, they are trained
fan-wise. All side shoots are then shortened
and after the spur system has formed no
further pruning should be required.

CHAMAECYPARIS **(false
cypress)** E C There are many species and a
great number of cultivars of varying sizes,

Fig. 7.5. *Clematis* × *jackmanii*

shapes and colour; no attempt to prune to shape should be made. Many of these cvs produce several leaders, which can easily be overlooked when the tree is young for then they in no way spoil the shape and are usually hidden by foliage. In their early years these are no trouble, but with age the leaders fall away and spoil the outline; surreptitious wiring is necessary to pull them together. The dwarf and small-growing kinds kind no pruning.

CHIMONANTHUS (winter sweet)

DS Although fully hardy this shrub does not flower freely unless the wood is properly ripened. For this reason, and to obtain some protection for its flowers during the winter, it is usually grown against a wall. Trained fanwise, the framework is tied to supports, and all branches coming away from the wall are removed. In July all side branches are cut back to two or three buds of the main framework. In a wet summer any excess growth should be thinned at the end of August to encourage better ripening.

Free-standing shrubs are trained to several leaders and all side shoots are shortened back to two or three buds in July.

CHOISYA (Mexican orange) ES
This shrub may be damaged in a colder-than-average winter, so plant in a position protected from cold winds. Dead-head following flowering trimming to shape at the same time.

CISTUS
ES All species are tender to some extent, needing full sun and a well-drained, not too rich soil. Following flowering, remove dead flowers and their stems as well as any winter damage, and trim to shape.

CLADRASTIS
D T A large-growing tree which should be trained to a single leader and feathered. The wood tends to be brittle and a mature tree can shed limbs, so during training space well the main branches and do not allow undue extension.

CLEMATIS
D/E CL If space permits, these climbers can be left to their own devices with a minimum of pruning; most of the species are treated in this way (Fig. 7.5).

They fall more or less into two groups. Those flowering on current season's growth, eg the × *jackmanii*, *lanuginosa* and *viticella* groups. These can be cut down to ground-level in February. To extend the flowering season, some stems can be left unpruned either in their entirety or reduced in length. These shoots should be removed completely in the following year.

The second group flowers on short growth from stems produced in the previous year. Included here are the *patens*, *florida* and *montana* groups. These are pruned after flowering, when shoots which have carried flowers are removed and there is a thinning of excess growth. The *florida* and *patens* groups sometimes produce a late flush of flowers and such shoots are reduced following flowering.

One or two species such as *C. recta* and *C. heracleifolia* are non-climbers; the former is usually cut to ground-level each February whilst the second is cut back to a framework.

CLERODENDRUM D S All species
are tender and even the hardiest are frequently cut back in a cold winter though they break away again readily from below ground-level. Cut out winter damage and reduce the shoots in May.

CLETHRA D/E S The deciduous species
are hardier than the evergreen and have a suckering habit; there should be a thinning out of shoots at ground-level in March. The evergreen group need a favoured position to succeed and are usually trained to a single leader but all side shoots are retained.

CLIANTHUS (lobster claw) E S *C. puniceus*
is a sprawling tender shrub that needs the support and protection of a south wall. Following spring blooming remove those shoots which have borne flowers. Seed set can be heavy and if these are left to ripen the vigour of the plant declines.

COLLETIA L S All species are slightly
tender and need a warm position. Cut out discoloured shoots after flowering, or in May for the late flowerers, and judiciously trim to keep tidy.

COLUTEA (bladder senna) D S/T If
it is to be grown as a tree, train to a single leader and feather. Following the formation of a framework, some thinning may be necessary and trimming of the branches will remove the old seed pods. If space is limited or if they are growing beyond their allotted space they can be cut hard back periodically in winter. When grown as a shrub, train to three leaders. During the winter months cut back hard to a framework and thin out growth from the centre of the bush.

CONVOLVULUS E S *C. cneorum* is
slightly tender and needs planting in a warm sunny position. Thin out shoots in April and trim to shape.

CORNUS D S For pruning purposes this
genus can be divided into those that sucker and those that develop a single stem. The former tend to make clumps and these should be thinned out during the winter when all shoots which have carried fruit can be removed. A number of these shrubs have attractively coloured stems which are cut to ground-level annually in March.

A single leader should be selected for the kinds which become trees; side shoots should be reduced but retained as long as possible.

CORONILLA E S Some species are
tender and need protection. Prune in April, trimming back shoots to about half their length.

CORYLOPSIS D S Flowers are produced
during the winter on one-year-old wood. No pruning is necessary unless one wishes to restrict growth, in which case prune after flowering.

CORYLUS (hazel) D S/T A few species
are tree-like and these are trained to a central leader and feathered. Suckering along the trunk is common and these should be rubbed off whilst still soft in May. Mostly the species are shrub-like with a strong tendency to sucker; these are trimmed after flowering to restrict them, and the suckers are also removed. *C. avellana*, the hazel, and *C. maxima*, the filbert or cob, are grown in coppices for their nuts, and *C. avellana* may be cut down to ground-level every few years for brushwood. Both the hazel and cobnut are grown in

gardens for their winter catkins; some trimming is needed following flowering. Both have purple-leaved forms which are pruned quite hard after flowering.

COTINUS (smokebush) E S *C. coggygria* and *obovatus* may still be better known under their classification of *Rhus*. If grown for their smoky flowers there is little pruning except to thin out crowded shoots and to tip shoots in the winter months. When growing the purple-leaved forms of either species for autumn colour, hard pruning in the winter months can be practised.

COTONEASTER E/D S/T The strongest growing kinds such as *C. frigida* can be trained to a single leader and feathered so as to form trees. There are one or two pendulous forms such as *C. salicifolia* which can be trained as weeping standards. A single leader is trained up a stake and all side shoots pinched back until there is a clear 1·8m (6ft) stem. Sometimes they are high grafted on to a 1·8m (6ft) stem. Cut back all side shoots in April and train in a well-spaced framework.

Cotoneasters grown as shrubs only require thinning and restriction of growth; evergreens are pruned in April and the deciduous kinds in winter. The prostrate forms which are used as ground cover benefit from an occasional thinning to let in the light. One or two species such as *C. horizontalis*, lend themselves to training against an east- or north-facing wall. Form a well-spaced framework, removing any branches which come away from the wall and thinning out the young branches without destroying the grace of the natural habit.

Fireblight is a troublesome disease with this genus.

CRATAEGUS (thorns) D S/T Almost all kinds will form small trees if trained to a single leader and feathered; they are, being small in stature, well suited to training as standards. Following training, the only pruning necessary is to remove crossing branches and to thin out during the winter months.

Those to be trained as shrubs can have three leaders. Subsequent pruning consists of keeping the centre of the bush open and carrying out judicious thinning in March.

This genus is susceptible to fireblight disease, the symptoms of which are most obvious in June.

CUNNINGHAMIA E C Train to a single leader, retaining most of the side branches as long as possible. These are produced copiously and some thinning may be desirable. In some forms there is a multiplicity of leaders formed and trying to restrict to one alone is virtually impossible. Such specimens should be trained as shrubs but their centres should be cleared of the mass of dead and weak shoots in April.

× CUPRESSOCYPARIS E C *C.* × *leylandii* is a fast growing hybrid conifer which is well anchored and is much planted in exposed conditions for windbreaks. Plant shrubs from open ground rather than from containers. Select and retain a single leader.

CUPRESSUS (cypress) E C Most species are somewhat tender. Select and retain a single leader, shortening back the side branches on the kinds that spread. In general no trimming is necessary and all side shoots should be retained as long as possible.

CYDONIA (quince) D S Suckers are freely produced so it is better to train the framework on a short leg. Flowering is on spurs and once established no pruning is necessary, but in the early years side shoots can be shortened back to two or three buds from the framework. Ensure that the centre of the bush is kept open.

CYTISUS (broom) D S Prune after flowering, cutting back to where new shoots are breaking. Avoid cutting into old wood. At the same time cut out crowded shoots and open up the centre of the bush.

C. battandieri is so different from other brooms that one may be excused for thinking it a different genus. It is slightly tender and often grown against a wall. Either as a wall shrub or free standing, it needs little pruning except for cutting out winter damage in April. Thin and cut out some of the old wood occasionally.

DABOECIA (St Dabeoc's heath)
E S Shear over the bushes in April, taking off old flower stalks and most of the last year's growth; trim to shape at the same time.

DAPHNE
E/D S In general these shrubs are left unpruned. *D. mezereum* is an exception for if left unpruned it becomes gaunt with long bare stems. Each spring remove those twigs which have carried the flowers. If the prostrate kinds develop long bare stems, these should be pegged down and covered with soil: they will root and, in time, form dense clumps.

DAVIDIA (handkerchief tree)
D T Select a single leader and reduce the side shoots, gradually removing them until there is a clear stem of the desired length.

DECAISNEA
D S This shrub has a stool-like habit, developing upright shoots which last for several years. When these become gaunt and bare they should be removed by cutting off at ground-level in autumn. Young growth is liable to damage from late frosts and if so affected should be trimmed with a knife.

DEUTZIA
D S Pruning follows flowering, when the shoots which have carried flowers are removed. Open up the centre of the bush and cut out shoots that are crowded.

D. scabra is a strong upright grower and has the added attraction of an interesting bark. Leave unpruned, carrying out judicious thinning only.

DIERVILLA
D S Following flowering, cut back to where new growth is breaking and thin.

DIOSPYROS
D S/T The strong-growing forms are trained to a single leader with side branches shortened but retained as long as possible. The less vigorous kinds can be allowed to remain as shrubs, trained to a single leader or to several. *D. kaki*, the persimmon, is often grown against a wall where the benefit of the extra warmth helps in the ripening of the fruit. Train the main framework as a fan and shorten back the laterals in April.

DIPELTA
D S All are strong upright growers which are best left unpruned for their barks provide some interest during the winter. When pruning is necessary, eg in the small garden or when restriction is desirable, do this after flowering, and cut back to where new growth is breaking.

ELAEAGNUS (oleaster)
D/E S/T The strongest growers can be trained as small trees by selecting a single leader and feathering. Later pruning is to thin and trim. The less vigorous growers are allowed several leaders and trained as shrubs. Most are grown for their foliage and all benefit from annual pruning. Deciduous kinds should have side shoots cut hard back in March and the centres of the bush kept open. Evergreens should be pruned in April when they may be thinned and trimmed to shape. As some of the variegated forms have a tendency to revert any plain green shoots should be removed at their point of origin.

EMBOTHRIUM (Chilean fire-bush)
D S These shrubs and trees are sensitive to soil and atmospheric conditions and if these are unfavourable growth will be unsatisfactory. Pruning is undesirable and confined to correcting misshapen branches after flowering.

ENKIANTHUS
D S Carry out dead-heading, thinning at the same time.

ERICA (heath)
E S Only the European species are commonly grown in gardens and one or two of these are tender. Annual pruning is necessary to keep the clumps tidy, compact and floriferous. Using shears, remove old flowers and most of the previous year's growth; the winter and spring flowerers should be clipped after flowering and the summer and autumn flowerers in February. Those with coloured foliage can be cut again as the flowers form, for flower and foliage colour do not always blend.

ERIOBOTRYA (loquat)
D T *E. japonica* rarely produces ripe fruit in Britain. As flowering takes place in the autumn and the fruit does not ripen until the next summer, few fruits in fact survive the winter. The loquat is

too large to train against a wall but it is grown as a free-standing small tree for its attractive, large, dark-green leaves. Pruning consists of removing any blackened foliage and thinning in April.

ESCALLONIA E S Whilst generally considered to be tender, most, especially the hybrids, will survive all but the coldest winters. Flowering is on current season's growth and once a framework has been formed, prune hard to within two or three buds of this in April. In cold districts and for the definitely tender species wall cultivation is necessary. After training a well-spaced fan of branches, cut back all laterals hard in May.

EUCALYPTUS E T Only a few species of this large family are sufficiently hardy for cultivation in this country. Failure is most often due to poor siting and planting of specimens that are too large and root-bound. Plant small container-grown specimens in an open site but protected from cold winds. A mass of shoots will be produced on the sapling, but eventually one will develop more strongly to become a leader whilst the remaining side shoots will die away. Later, branches are shed to leave a clean bole.

Eucalyptus has two stages of growth, juvenile and adult; the shape and colour of leaves at each stage may be quite different. Foliage is much in demand by the floral arranger, the juvenile foliage usually being the more popular. Cutting of foliage can take place at any time of the year except when in active growth, but excessive cutting should be avoided during the winter months. When adult shoots are cut the new ones arising will be juvenile and a tree can be kept in this state indefinitely by regular hard pruning in early May.

EUONYMUS (spindle tree) D/E S/T A few species will make trees and these are kept to a single leader, the side branches being shortened and gradually removed. The shrubby kinds are allowed several leaders and in general little pruning is necessary except to thin, trim and keep the centres of the bush open.

The deciduous kinds are sometimes grown primarily for their autumn colour and these can be pruned more severely to encourage strong young growth; this is carried out in March. The best known evergreen is *E. japonicus*, of which there are many variegated forms, some of them very prone to reversion. This species, which is grown mainly for its foliage, is trimmed to shape at the same time as the other evergreens are pruned, in April. This species is very prone to attacks by mildew which can become so bad that normal spraying gives little control. If this happens, severe pruning will remove the unsightly foliage, and the new growth, it is to be hoped, will stay clean.

EUPHORBIA E S Whilst most of this genus is herbaceous, a number are woody. These produce upright, rather succulent stems copiously from a rootstock. After flowering cut out at ground-level all shoots which have flowered and all weak stems. When growth is not strong carry out dead-heading, cutting out completely some of the oldest stems.

EXOCHORDA D S These have a suckering habit and are best trained on a short leg before branching is permitted. Pruning, when necessary, should follow flowering; thin crowded shoots and trim to shape.

FAGUS (beech) D T Often slow-growing in the years following planting, but when once established there is plenty of vigour. Select a central leader, and feather. Weeping varieties are grafted and a leader should be trained up a stake until there is a sufficient length of trunk.

× FATSHEDERA (fatheaded Lizzy) E S *F. lizei* is a bigeneric hybrid which has a sprawling habit and may be trained up a north or east wall or used as ground cover. Pruning is rarely necessary (Fig. 7.6).

FATSIA E S Remove dead leaves in April and cut out any bare gaunt stems at ground-level (Fig. 7.7).

FORSYTHIA D S Hard pruning encourages growth at the expense of flowering so annual pruning should be no more than the

Fig. 7.6. × *Fatshedera lizei*

Fig. 7.7. *Fatsia japonica*

removal of crowded shoots from the centre of the bush and a proportion of the oldest wood. When pruning an old or an extra large shrub spread the operation over three years; begin by removing the oldest wood after flowering.

F. suspensa is often grown against a wall where its long pendulous shoots are displayed to better advantage. A well-spaced fan-shaped framework is trained and tied and from this will develop the long weeping stems. These are all cut hard back to the framework following flowering. When desired as free-standing shrubs, several are planted together so as to give each other support. After planting, reduce the shoots by half or even more; the following winter cut back to where they begin to curve over. Once a rigid framework has been formed shoots can be allowed to develop freely; subsequent pruning is to remove some or all of the shoots which have flowered.

FOTHERGILLA D S Slow-growing shrubs of bushy habit which need little pruning. Old shoots which become gaunt and un-

tidy should be removed completely following flowering.

FRAXINUS (ash) D T Train to a single leader and feather. Train in a new leader if the original is lost, remembering that because of opposite buds two will develop where there was one. Weeping forms must have the leader tied to a stake; a clear 3·6m (12ft) stem should be produced before a framework is developed.

FUCHSIA D S Only a few species are hardy enough for cultivation out of doors all the year round in Britain. Even those can be cut down in a cold winter but the bushes usually break away freely from ground-level. In April prune back all one-year shoots almost to ground-level or to a framework (Fig. 7.8).

GARRYA (tassel bush) E S Male and female flowers are produced on different plants and it is the male kind with the long catkins that is grown in gardens. Pruning consists of thinning and trimming to shape in April.

Fig. 7.8. *Fuchsia*

Although hardy if given protection against cold winds, it is frequently planted against a wall where there is some protection for the winter catkins which then grow longer. After training in a well-spaced framework, some trimming should be carried out in April.

GAULTHERIA E S Many species are
small growing or prostrate and need almost no pruning. Even the taller kinds require little attention beyond cutting out some of the oldest wood and trimming to shape in April. *G. shallon* is often used as game or ground cover and if it becomes untidy it can be cut hard in April.

GENISTA L S Pruning is generally unnecessary except to dead-head and trim to shape at the same time.

GINKGO (maidenhair tree) D C
There are many different forms of *G. biloba*. It is important to see that pruning is related to the habit of the tree for it is not really possible to change the type of growth. Train to a single leader and feather, taking out strong branches which tend to develop low down on the tree.

GRISELINIA (broadwood) E S *G. littoralis* is considered to be hardy except in the coldest districts, although there does seem to be a variation in hardiness amongst different forms. Trim to shape in April.

HALESIA D T/S Strong growers that will make trees if restricted to a central leader, when feathering will be beneficial. Often trained as large shrubs, when several leaders may be allowed. Annual pruning is minimal and consists of removing crossing branches and keeping the centres of bushes open.

HALIMIUM E S All species are more or less tender requiring a warm sunny position in well-drained, not too rich soil. Following flowering, cut out those shoots which have carried flowers and trim to shape.

HAMAMELIS (witch hazel) D S
Pruning is generally unnecessary. Most kinds offered for sale are grafted, so watch for suckers; as these closely resemble the desired plant remove all shoots coming from below ground-level.

H. japonica arborea will make a small tree if trained to a single leader; shorten the lower shoots but retain them as long as possible.

HEBE E S A large family of shrubs from New Zealand of varying hardiness, size and form, often as important for foliage as for flower. A number of species are tender, eg *H. hulkeana*, and should be planted at the foot of a south wall. Those that flower early in the year are pruned after flowering when all shoots which have carried flowers are cut out and there is some trimming. Autumn-flowerers are pruned in May when shortening of the shoots is practised and some thinning.

The hardy kinds need little attention except a trimming to shape in April.

HEDERA (ivy) E CL Ivy comes to mind at once when it is a matter of trying to decide on a climber for a wall. It can, however, be invasive and if left unattended can dislodge slates, gutters and down-pipes.

Ivy has two stages of growth: the juvenile with angular leaves and climbing roots, and the later stage when side branches without roots are produced, leaves become rounder and flowering takes place. It can be slow to start growing up a wall. Train a well-balanced framework, paying attention to clothing, especially at the base of the wall. Cut well back from windows, doors, pipes, gutters and the roof. If branches develop, cut them back close to the wall. It is only on young shoots that roots develop which adhere to the wall and if these die or are wrenched away, there is no hold. Each year cut out some of the oldest wood so that the ivy does not with age become so heavy that it falls away from the wall.

Controversy has long raged as to whether ivy growing up a tree is harmful to it. As long as the tree is in good health no damage is done.

HIBISCUS D S Mainly a tropical genus; only one species, *H. syriacus*, is commonly seen in British gardens. This flowers on current season's growth, and once a framework has been trained all young shoots are cut back to within a few buds of it in April. Coral spot can be troublesome, especially if the shrub is weak.

HIPPOPHAË (sea buckthorn) D S/T
Male and female flowers are borne on separate
bushes and so to obtain berries they should be
planted in groups with one male to four or five
females. Though most often grown as shrubs,
they make small trees if trained to a single
leader with the lower side shoots reduced.
Little pruning is required except to trim and
thin during the dormant season.

HOHERIA D/ES All species are tender to
some extent and are frequently trained against
a wall in all but the mildest districts. Once
trained, only removal of winter damage, thinning and trimming in May are required. *H.
lyallii* and *glabrata* are the hardiest species and
may be grown as free-standing shrubs, but
even these can be damaged in a cold winter
especially following a wet autumn when wood
does not ripen properly. During April, cut out
winter damage and reduce growth by about
half.

HYDRANGEA E/D S/CL Hydrangeas often take a year or two to settle down before
they start to flower regularly. In general they
are little pruned except to dead-head and thin
out growth in April.

Climbing hydrangeas attach themselves to
their support by means of roots, and as with
ivy there are two stages—juvenile growth with
climbing roots which clings tight to its support.
In the adult stage, branches develop which
have no roots and these bear flowers. These
flowering shoots are cut back hard in April.

H. macrophylla, the common hydrangea,
flowers on one-year wood and pruning consists
of the removal of all, or part of the shoot which
has flowered and the cutting out of weak
shoots. In wet seasons a more drastic thinning
may be necessary to help ripen the wood. The
old flower heads are often of interest throughout the winter and, as in cold districts they give
protection to overwintering flowerbuds, pruning can be delayed until April. A few kinds,
eg *H. paniculata*, flower on current season's
growth and these are cut hard back to a framework or to ground-level during March.

HYPERICUM (St John's wort) D S
A few species are tender. Flowers are produced on current season's growth and in
April all shoots are cut to within a few inches
of the ground. Larger plants can be produced
by thinning and tipping the young growth.

ILEX (holly) E/D S/T Hollies are often
slow to establish but having done so, grow
away strongly. The strong growers which are
to become trees should have a single leader
selected but all side shoots retained until they
die naturally. Pruning consists of trimming to
shape in April. Neglected hollies or those dis-
figured by leaf miner can be cut back in April
or in July. It is preferable to carry out this
operation over two or three years rather than
all at once.

JASMINUM E/D CL/S Some species are
tender and need protection. Both the climbers
and free-standing shrubs need little pruning
except to remove some of the wood which has
flowered. This can be carried out after flowering with most, but for those that flower over
a long period pruning should be done in April.
J. nudiflorum should be pruned after flowering,
removing most of the wood that has flowered.
This increases flowering and keeps the climber
tidier.

JUGLANS (walnut) D T Train to a
central leader and feather. Prune when in leaf,
since the tree 'bleeds' less then. Young growth
is susceptible to damage by late frosts which
may necessitate trimming and retraining of a
leader.

JUNIPERUS (juniper) E C Some
forms make trees and these should be trained
to a central leader, with all side shoots retained.
The bushes can have several leaders but in
April the centres should be cleared of the clutter of shoots, dead and alive. Dwarf and prostrate junipers are not pruned.

KALMIA (calico bush) E S Very little
pruning except for dead-heading. When
bushes become straggly or there is an excess
of old wood, hard pruning can be practised
during April.

KERRIA D S Flowers are produced on the
previous year's growth of bright green stems,
so attractive in winter. Kerria has a suckering

habit, forming large clumps which may need to be restricted. Cut out old canes at ground-level as flowers fade.

KOELREUTERIA D S/T A strong grower often trained as a tree when a central leader is selected and the lower branches retained as long as possible though reduced. The plant is not normally pruned when grown as a shrub.

KOLKWITZIA (beauty bush) D S This bush can be left to develop naturally except for the thinning of shoots where crowded. If, however, space is limited, annual pruning can be carried out in June when shoots which have flowered are cut out.

× LABURNOCYTISUS D T Flowers should be pink, but on the same tree yellow laburnum flowers and purple broom flowers also appear. At flowering time cut away the shoots bearing yellow flowers for these grow away at the expense of those with pink flowers which will decline unless given this assistance.

LABURNUM (golden chain) D T Most commonly grown as small trees and often trained as standards, for which they are well suited, although a central leader is to be preferred. Strong vertical shoots tend to appear from low down on the tree and these should be removed as they appear.

Laburnum responds well to spur pruning so that trees can be restricted in size by cutting back side shoots to two or three buds in the winter; they are well suited to pleaching. The trees seed heavily and the immature seed pods should be removed, especially as the seed is poisonous.

LARIX (larch) D C Select a single leader, replacing if damaged by pest or weather, and retain all side branches as long as possible. Prune when fully dormant. Late pruning results in excessive gumming.

LAURUS (bay) E S/T Slightly tender and susceptible to damage from low temperatures or exposure to cold winds. Train to a central leader, retaining all side branches as long as possible. Bays are commonly seen trimmed, an operation which is carried out in April.

LAVANDULA (lavender) E S A few species are tender and need the base of a warm south wall. These are trimmed to shape in May, when winter damage is cut out.

Common lavender is frequently seen in gardens as an untidy sprawling bush, due entirely to lack of pruning. During April, just prior to growth commencing, bushes should be clipped hard, in the course of which old flower spikes are removed and most of the previous year's growth. Neglected bushes need very hard pruning but it is better done in two or three stages and not all at once.

LAVATERA (tree mallow) D S Slightly tender shrubs needing full sun and a rather poor, well-drained soil. Trim to shape in April.

LEDUM E S Pruning should be unnecessary except to thin and to remove dead wood. If this becomes excessive it is an indication that all is not well.

LEIOPHYLLUM E S Classed with the heathers which it closely resembles, it is treated in the same way. Trim over with a pair of shears in March.

LEPTOSPERMUM (tea tree) E S *L. scoparium* is the hardiest species and this can be damaged by excessive cold; all other species are tender. Most species and the coloured forms of *L. scoparium* are grown against a south wall. Pruning is best carried out after flowering, when wood which has flowered is removed together with any winter damage. Some thinning of blind shoots is desirable.

LEUCOTHOË E S Occasionally it may be necessary to remove at ground-level old wood and any unsightly stems in April.

LEYCESTERIA D S One species is tender and only suited to a warm wall. *L. formosa* is planted for game cover but is also an attractive addition to a garden for flowers, fruit and stem colour. It has a stool-like habit and

the old stems are cut out in April. If growth is strong, the entire clump can be cut down to ground-level each year.

LIGUSTRUM (privet) E/D S Privets

are best known as hedging plants though specimens are sometimes used in topiary. Grown for foliage, flowers or fruit they can make handsome shrubs or even small trees. Shrubs are left to develop several leaders and established pruning consists of trimming to shape and thinning in March. Strong-growing forms can be trained to a single leader with all side shoots retained but shortened, and eventually removed.

LIPPIA D S A tender shrub in most parts of

the British Isles and usually given wall protection. Even there, it may be cut back in a cold winter. Pruning is carried out in May when the previous year's shoots are shortened almost to a mature framework.

LIQUIDAMBAR D T Select a strong

central leader and feather. Strong branches can occur low down on the tree and these should be removed.

LIRIODENDRON (tulip tree) D T

Select a central leader and feather. Remove any strong upright growth which begins from low down on the tree; the bark is easily damaged if blunt tools are used and such wood tends to die back. Training and subsequent pruning is best carried out in July or August.

LONICERA (honeysuckle) D/E S/CL

Shrubby honeysuckles after flowering, should be trimmed to shape and branches which have flowered cut back or removed completely. If a feature is to be made of the berries, pruning should be delayed until the winter, or April for evergreens.

It is not necessary to prune climbers every year unless space is restricted. Climbers can be separated into two groups: those flowering on current season's growth are pruned in the winter, when necessary, cutting back hard to a framework; those flowering on one-year-old wood are pruned after flowering when those shoots which have flowered are removed, together with crowded growth.

LUPINUS (lupin) E S Mostly herbace-

ous but there are one or two shrubby species of which the best known is *L. arboreus*. Select a site in full sun in a well-drained, not too rich soil. Dead-head and trim to shape annually.

LEYCIUM (box thorn) D S All species

are slightly tender and liable to damage in a cold winter, so are more commonly grown by the sea. Bushes tend to sprawl, a condition aggravated by too good planting conditions or by planting in shade. Trim drastically to shape in April and thin.

MAGNOLIA E/D S/T Branches tend to be

pithy and bark is easily damaged if blunt or badly set tools are used. Pruning is best carried out in July when new growth is complete: dormant wood is slow to heal and die-back following winter pruning is common.

Tree magnolias should be kept to a single leader on which the side shoots are shortened and eventually removed. Young growth is frequently damaged by late frosts and if the leader is destroyed a new one will have to be trained in.

M. grandiflora is still considered as a wall shrub but is really unsuitable in such a position for its large leaves cause undue shading, and with age the trunks become increasingly difficult to keep tied back. Wall-trained *M. grandiflora* does perhaps flower more abundantly than a free-standing tree so if training is undertaken for this reason a well-spaced framework must be provided. This can be fan-shaped or in tiers, ensuring that the base of the wall is kept clothed. Established pruning means removing old fruits and thinning and cutting back shoots coming from the wall in July.

Bush magnolia need little attention, although dead-heading is desirable for many kinds produce copious quantities of fruit which, if left to develop, reduce vigour. When dead-heading, cut rather than break off the spent flowers for the new growth buds are just behind the flowers. *M. soulangiana* varieties have a tendency to produce masses of young growth along the main stem; this should be rubbed off as it appears.

MAHONIA E S Several of the low-grow-

ing kinds can be used for ground cover, which

can be kept low and thick if sheared off just above ground-level every three or four years; if not growing strongly remove some of the oldest stems and trim back remaining growth. Other forms need only occasional pruning when the oldest stems are put out at ground-level in April.

MALUS (crab apple) D T Some species are raised from seed and therefore on their own roots, but many species and all cultivars are grafted on to one of the fruit rootstocks which controls the ultimate size of the tree. Most crab apples are trained as standards although they can also be trained to a central leader. Once the framework has formed, there is little pruning required beyond the removal of crossing branches.

MESPILUS (medlar) D T The enjoyment of the fruit of medlar is an acquired taste at present out of favour and this plant is now grown mainly as an ornamental. Once a framework has been formed, either as a standard or with a central leader, all that is necessary is to remove crossing branches.

MORUS (mulberry) D T Select a central leader and reduce all side shoots, gradually removing them. Once a framework has formed, all that is necessary is to remove crossing branches in autumn.

MYRICA E/D S Grown for fragrant foliage and wood, requiring only a trimming to shape in April.

MYRTUS (myrtle) E S All species are tender and need a sheltered garden if they are to be grown as completely free-standing shrubs or small trees. Select a central leader and reduce side shoots; retain these as long as possible, removing them if they become crowded. During May, trim to shape and thin out crowded shoots.

In colder areas, myrtle can be grown in the protection of a south wall, either planted close to it and trained against it, in tiers or as a fan, or planted a little way from the wall and allowed to grow free-standing but in its shelter. In May trim to shape and thin out crowded shoots, and remove winter damage.

NANDINA (heavenly bamboo) E S If old stems become gaunt and leaf size diminishes, they should be cut out at ground-level in April.

NEILLIA D S Shrubs with a stool-like habit. The oldest wood should be removed at ground-level during the winter months and tall stems reduced in height.

NOTHOFAGUS E/D T *N. procera* and *obliqua* are the hardiest species and fast growers, making large deciduous trees. Select a central leader and feather; the main branches in the crown should be well spaced.

Most species, being evergreen, are tender and really only suited to the milder parts of Britain. Select a central leader but retain all side shoots for as long as possible.

NYSSA D S/T In areas where these thrive, they will form trees and as such should be trained to a central leader which is feathered. Often grown in gardens as large shrubs when they can be permitted several leaders or again restricted to a single leader but with all side shoots retained. Annual trimming or even judicious removal of branches to restrict growth can be practised in early spring where space is limited.

OLEA (olive) E S/T Tender and needs a sheltered garden in a mild area to succeed. When free-standing it is usually trained to a single leader; side shoots are shortened and retained as long as possible. Some thinning may be necessary. In less favoured gardens it is trained against a wall for protection, either tiered or fanwise. In May cut back shoots coming away from the wall, thin out growth, and trim to shape.

OLEARIA E S/T Most species are tender and are often planted as free-standing shrubs at the foot of a wall. *O. haastii* and *O. macrodonta* are two of the hardiest species, needing no protection. Those which flower early in the year are pruned after flowering when old flower shoots are removed and the bush is trimmed to shape. Those flowering late are pruned in May, again old flower stalks are removed and bushes are trimmed to shape.

OSMANTHUS E S/T Most species are tender and need wall protection. *O. delavayi* and *O. heterophyllus* are the hardiest, the former flowering in spring, the latter in late autumn. The early flowerers are trimmed after flowering, the late flowerers in May just before growth begins. × *Osmarea burkwoodii* is now to be called *Osmanthus* × *burkwoodii*. This should be trimmed to shape after flowering.

OSMARONIA D S Has a suckering habit and eventually forms large clumps. This shrub, which flowers early in the year, should have the oldest stems, and any weak ones, removed after flowering.

OSTRYA D T Select a central leader and reduce side shoots, gradually removing them. Carry out pruning when tree is fully dormant; delayed pruning results in bleeding.

PACHYSANDRA E S Widely grown for ground cover. Pruning is only necessary if stems become bare and woody or foliage thin. Shear over a few inches above ground-level in April.

PAEONIA (tree peony) D S Most species are herbaceous, only a few having woody stems. Occasionally take out some of the old stems at ground-level if they become gaunt; remove dead flowers and fruiting heads after flowering; if seeds are wanted, delay until these have been shed. Towards the end of a wet summer some thinning of lush growth will aid the ripening of wood.

PALIURUS D S An untidy grower which should be trimmed to shape and thinned out in March.

PARROTIA D S A shrub for its early flowers and colourful bark, but particularly for its gorgeous autumn colour. A strong-growing shrub which can become a tree of considerable size although the form usually seen in Britain makes one that is of medium size with a flat top. It can be trained to a central leader with all side shoots retained, or it can be allowed to develop naturally. If a feature is to be made of the trunk, feathering must be practised until a clear trunk of sufficient length has been obtained. *Parrotia persica* produces masses of branches which should be thinned in winter or following flowering. Cut back to a point where there is another branch.

PARTHENOCISSUS D CL This genus now contains the virginia creeper (*P. tricuspidata* or as it is probably better known, *Ampelopsis veitchii*). All are vigorous climbers which attach themselves to supports by means of tendrils on which there are suckers. Unless given plenty of space (as on an old tree) they can be invasive, shutting out light from windows and dislodging slates, gutters and down pipes. Where possible an annual reduction of growth is desirable, at the least cutting well back from windows, doors, pipes, gutters and roof. Cut out old wood in winter, remembering that it is only young shoots which are able to attach themselves to supports.

PASSIFLORA (passion flower) D/ E CL All species are tender and even *P. caerulea*, the hardiest, can be damaged by winter cold. Train a well-spaced framework to cover a wall, then thin out crowded growth and drastically reduce during May (Fig. 7.9).

PAULOWNIA D T These are fast growing when young, producing rather succulent pithy shoots which are easily damaged by cold, especially when not properly ripened. Flower buds are formed in the autumn and carried through the winter with a high mortality rate, survivors opening in late spring. It is only in the mildest parts of Britain that regular flowering can be expected so the tree is often grown for its foliage.

Little pruning is necessary except for the removal of winter damage and dead wood followed by some thinning; this is carried out in April or following flowering. During training select a central leader and retrain a new one if damaged by frost. Aim to produce a well-balanced framework for the wood is rather brittle.

Young shoots that are well fed grow strongly and produce very large heart-shaped leaves. A feature can be made of these shoots with their spectacular foliage as in tropical bedding or in cold gardens where space is limited.

Fig. 7.9. *Passiflora*

PERIPLOCA D CL An untidy, strong climber that needs trimming to shape in March, with thinning and the removal of weak shoots.

PERNETTYA E S A suckering shrub grown for its attractive show of fruits which remain largely untouched by birds. In good conditions it can become rather invasive and some restriction may be desirable; otherwise occasionally remove some of the oldest wood in April.

PEROWSKIA D S Shoots of this shrub often die back to a rootstock in the winter, and as flowers are on current season's growth, the remaining shoots are cut back to ground-level in March.

PHILADELPHUS (mock orange) D S If there is plenty of space, these shrubs can be grown with the minimum of pruning, removing blind shoots from the centre of the bush and reducing surplus shoots. When space is limited remove branches that have carried flowers and thin out surplus shoots in July.

PHILLYREA E S Trim to shape and thin out if crowded, after flowering.

PHLOMIS E S Only some species are woody and most of these are slightly tender, needing full sun and a warm position. Cut out or cut back old flowering stems and thin growth in spring.

PHOTINIA E S Some species are somewhat tender and are often grown on a south wall. Valued more for their young red foliage than for their flowers which are not very interesting. In April all growth is trimmed back to about half of that produced in the previous year.

PHYGELIUS D S The tops are often killed in the winter and, in the manner of herbaceous plants, growth is produced from beneath ground-level. If the tops do survive they should be cut away, for flowering is on current season's growth.

PHYSOCARPUS D S Strong-growing shrubs with a stool-like habit. Cut out the

80

oldest shoots, and any that are thin or weak, during the winter. If grown for foliage cut hard to within a few inches of the ground in March.

PICEA (spruce) E C Select and retain a central leader, keeping all side shoots as long as possible.

PIERIS E S Little pruning is necessary except to dead-head, thin and trim. Young non-flowering growth of *P. forrestii* is a brilliant red which fades green as it ages. A second flush of brilliant growth can be obtained by the (unorthodox) practice of trimming back the shoots when the leaves have turned green.

PINUS (pine) E C Some of the naturally dwarf forms such as *P. pumila* produce several leaders, but in general all species should be kept to a single leader which should be re-trained if damaged by weather or insects. Prune when fully dormant to avoid excessive gumming.

PITTOSPORUM E S Most species are tender, *P. tenuifolium* being the hardiest of them. Plant in a protected place out of cold winds. Trim to shape in April, cutting out winter damage and thinning.

PLATANUS (plane) D T Fast-growing trees, commonly used in street planting and there often spoilt by lopping. Given plenty of space, they make graceful trees and with age branches sweep to the ground. Select a central leader and feather, aiming to produce a trunk with a clear stem of 15ft with a well-balanced and spaced framework.

PODOCARPUS E S/T The smaller-growing kinds tend to be hardier than the tree-forms. The former may be trimmed to shape in April, and the latter, in sheltered gardens, are trained to a single leader.

POLYGONUM D CL Mostly non-woody plants of which *P. baldschuanicum*, the Russian vine, is an exception; this is a vigorous and fast-growing climber which is commonly grown for screening. Its rampant habit makes it ideal for this purpose but it does need plenty of space. Each year, in March, remove shoots that are likely to encroach, drastically reduce and thin out, cutting as near to the ground as possible.

POPULUS (poplar) D T Most species are strong growers when young. Select a central leader and feather. If pruning is necessary, carry out in the fully dormant period or bleeding may result. As canker disease, causing die-back and gumming, is troublesome in some parts of Britain all pruning cuts should be sealed. Take care not to damage roots otherwise suckering occurs.

POTENTILLA D S Untidy growers that tend to collect dead leaves and accumulate a mass of dead or blind twigs. Clear out centres of bushes in March and reduce the previous year's growth by a half.

PRUNUS D/E S/T There are many kinds of *Prunus* of differing size, shape and habit, and all of them are susceptible to silver leaf disease. Pruning of most species is kept to a minimum after building up a framework. Those which make trees are trained to a central leader and feathered.

Japanese cherries are grafted, sometimes low down but most often on to stems of varying lengths. Heads are often one-sided and by judicious pruning this should be corrected so as to produce a well-spaced and balanced spread.

Ornamental peaches, almonds and their hybrids should have a portion of wood which has flowered removed in April. Sometimes they are fan-trained against a wall; after building up a framework, remove shoots which have flowered. *Prunus triloba, P. glandulosa* and their forms are also grown against walls, and following the completion of a well-spaced framework, all side shoots are cut hard back to this after flowering.

Some kinds, eg *P. serrula*, are grown for their barks. Train a central leader and feather so as to expose the trunk as soon as possible. There are a number of weeping forms of cherries of various species and cv groups. These may be low grafted but are most often grafted high. Support the main stem with a stake and ensure that there is sufficient length of trunk to allow the pendant branches to hang gracefully. If the main stem is not long enough train in a leader, reducing the framework until sufficient length has been gained, then train in a new framework. The evergreen species are most often grown as hedges though they can be grown as specimen plants. Keep to a single leader. Retain side shoots; trim to shape in April.

PSEUDOLARIX D C

If conditions suit this conifer it can become a tree and as such is trained to a central leader. More often it is grown as a bush with several leaders, in which case it is not pruned.

PSEUDOTSUGA (Douglas fir) E C

A strong grower of tiered habit which is trained to a single leader, retaining all side shoots as long as possible.

PTEROCARYA D T

A strong-growing tree, especially when young. Train to a central leader and feather. Retrain a new leader if the original is lost: young growth is susceptible to damage from late frosts. Prune when fully dormant for bleeding results if cuts are made once the sap has started to rise.

PUNICA (pomegranate) D S

A tender shrub which is grown against a wall for its attractive flowers; fruit rarely if ever ripens in Britain. Train a well-spaced framework and cut back young shoots in May, thinning where crowded (Fig. 7.10). There is a dwarf form which needs no pruning except to thin out crowded shoots occasionally.

PYRACANTHA (firethorn) E S

Grown against a north or east wall, for which its habit is well suited. During training select several leaders, spacing them wide enough apart to allow side branches to cover their allotted space without overcrowding. The main leaders should be secured in position, for though they keep close to the wall they tend to fall away with age. During April, cut back any shoots coming away from the wall, thin out crowded shoots and trim back. As the leaders become old, select and train in new ones; when these are established the old can be removed.

Pyracanthas are perfectly well suited for growing as free-standing shrubs: three or five

Fig. 7.10. Pomegranate, *Punica granatum*

leaders should be selected and well spaced. In April open up the centre of the bush, thin out crowded shoots and trim to shape.

PYRUS (pear) D T Train to a single leader and feather. No regular pruning is necessary beyond the removal of crossing branches. *P. salicifolia*, and especially its weeping form, need to have the leader secured to a stake and should be trained to a 2·4m (8ft) stem before a framework is allowed to develop.

All species of *Pyrus* are susceptible to fireblight.

QUERCUS (oak) D/E T Transplant when quite small as large specimens are difficult to establish. For deciduous species train to a central leader and feather; the evergreens also are trained to a central leader, the side branches being reduced but retained as long as possible. Ensure that the main limbs are well spaced and give a good shape to the crown. Many evergreens are tender and may suffer damage from cold; some trimming may be necessary in May to remove discoloured foliage.

RAPHIOLEPIS E S These are spreading, rather untidy growers which should be thinned and trimmed in April. They are often planted at the base of a wall for some are tender.

RHAMNUS D S In general these shrubs should be allowed to develop naturally, though a few of the stronger species can be trained to a central leader and feathered. During February thin crowded shoots; forms with fancy leaves can be trimmed back moderately hard.

RHODODENDRON E/D S Azaleas, which form a series among the *Rhododendron* species, are included here. There are very many species and hybrids of varying sizes, shapes, habits, shape of flowers and degrees of hardiness. It is important when transplanting to replant to the same depth as previously. Too deep planting has an adverse effect, causing a sickly appearance and the dying out of parts of the shrub.

Many hybrids and some species are grafted and any suckers which arise from the rootstock should be removed as they appear; if left they grow away at the expense of the plant. Carry out dead-heading annually and at the same time trim back any shoot growing out of alignment. With age, some rhododendrons become too tall, bare at the base, or their shape falls away; these can be cut back really hard after flowering.

Bud blast is a disease which kills the flower buds; remove and burn infected buds.

RHODOTYPOS D S Remove each year, following flowering, the oldest shoots and any that are weak.

RHUS D S/T Gardeners are warned that some species can cause a skin rash. People vary in their sensitivity to different species but *R. vernix, toxicodendron* and *succedanea* are most likely to cause irritation. When pruning any species of *Rhus*, wear thick gloves, cover all bare parts of the body and wear overalls.

Tree forms are kept to a single leader and feathered. Shrubs can be left unpruned, thinning out crowded shoots in March. *R. typhina* and *glabra* and their forms are usually grown mainly for their foliage, either summer or autumn; the amount and size can be increased by pruning in the winter to within a few inches of the ground or to a framework. (*R. cotinus* and *R. cotinoides*, see Cotinus.)

RIBES (currants) D/E S A few species are tender. Mostly they flower on one-year-old wood, and after flowering the shoots which have borne flowers are removed. Some form spurs and a framework should be formed on a short leg, and well spaced. During the winter open up the centre of the bush and cut back young growth to within two or three buds of the main stems. Evergreen kinds are little pruned except to thin, if required, in April.

ROBINIA D T Most species have thorns and sucker freely if their roots are damaged. The wood of some is brittle and trees may shed large limbs in gales. Train to a single leader and feather, ensuring that the main limbs are well spaced and do not extend unduly. Remove any strong shoots which develop low down on the tree.

ROMNEYA (tree poppy) E S Rather succulent, behaving often as an herbaceous plant with growth that dies back to a rootstock in winter. It is usually planted against the side of path because its roots like a cool soil, but has the disconcerting habit of disappearing from the place chosen for it and reappearing elsewhere. In March or April, just prior to the commencement of growth, reduce any surviving shoots and cut out any old ones.

ROSMARINUS (rosemary) E S Whilst reasonably hardy, rosemary may suffer in an extra cold winter, and prostrate forms, if left unsheltered, can be killed or seriously damaged in even averagely cold weather. Bushes can be trimmed to shape in April but it is preferable to wait until after the first flush of flowers is over.

RUBUS (brambles) D/E S A few of the evergreen species are tender and need wall protection. Most species have a stool-like or even suckering habit, but some of the deciduous kinds have canes of only two years' duration.

Brambles with coloured stems are cut to ground-level in March, and young growth drastically thinned out in established clumps. Species grown for their flowers or fruit are pruned during the winter. If stems are of two-year duration only, those shoots which have flowered are removed; if stems are longer lived, those which have flowered should be cut back.

RUSCUS (butcher's broom) L S Remove discoloured shoots and occasionally some of the old wood in April.

RUTA (rue) E S All species are slightly tender and likely to be damaged in a cold winter. All are short lived and replacements should be kept available for replanting. Common rue (*R. graveolens*) is an untidy grower and needs drastic thinning and trimming in May.

SALIX (willow) D S/T Willows vary from tiny shrubs to large trees, all liking a moist soil. Strong-growing kinds are trained to a single leader and feathered; smaller kinds can be similarly treated but with all side shoots retained although reduced. There is a tendency for branches to be damaged or lost in gales so space out the main branches; prevent undue extension and avoid narrow crotches.

Shrubs can be treated as already described or can be allowed several leaders. When willows are grown especially for catkins or foliage, best produced on young wood, cut hard back to within a few inches of the base of the previous year's growth, just before growth commences. When grown for their coloured stems, cut to ground-level or to within a few buds of a framework in March. Small growing and prostrate kinds are rarely pruned except to remove dead wood or to thin.

SALVIA E/D S Many salvias are herbaceous but a few are shrubby, and of these the majority are tender. These tender kinds should be planted near the base of a south wall, though even here in a cold winter the tops can be killed—new growth, however, invariably emerges from or below ground-level. For this group, any growth which survives the winter should be cut hard back in spring.

Common sage (*S. officinalis*) is widely grown in the herb garden for culinary use, though coloured leaf or flower forms may find their way into the flower garden. There are two groups of common sage: those which flower freely and others which flower not at all or but rarely. With the first, cut out all shoots which have flowered and trim to shape in June. The second are trimmed to shape in April when any flowering stems are also removed.

SAMBUCUS (elder) D S During the dormant season cut out old wood and any weak shoots, open up the centre and trim back young shoots. Elders with fancy leaves are cut down to ground-level or hard back to a framework.

SANTOLINA (lavender cotton) E S Fragrant shrub with grey-white leaves grown for its foliage rather than its yellow flowers which, however, have some attraction. Unpruned bushes sprawl untidily and are short lived. After flowering, the old flower stems should be removed and the bushes trimmed back. When growing just for foliage, trimming is carried out in April and most of the previous year's growth is removed; a second trimming is desirable as the flower buds appear.

SARCOCOCCA E S Restrict if clumps become invasive; otherwise just cut out old gaunt stems, or if clumps become untidy shear back to a few inches of ground-level in April.

SCHIZOPHRAGMA D CL A climber which supports itself by producing roots on its young shoots. Space out these shoots as they begin to grow, pointing them in the desired direction; if they grow wrongly they have to be pulled off the wall and cannot be made to refix themselves. Once the support has been covered, branching occurs and flowering begins. Old flower shoots should be removed in March, being cut back as near as possible to the main framework.

SENECIO E S Many species are tender and need protection of a wall; in May remove winter damage and thin out crowded shoots. Free-standing shrubs are similarly treated in April, when they are trimmed to shape, thinned, and old flower stalks removed.

SEQUOIA E C *S. sempervirens* makes a very large tree, needing plenty of room and protection from wind, for in exposed conditions they tend to lose their leaders and become stunted. Keep and retain a single leader and all side branches, removing any strong branches which develop low down on the tree.

SEQUOIADENDRON (giant redwood) E C *S. giganteum*, the world's largest tree should not be planted unless there is plenty of space for development and some protection from wind. Select a central leader and retain all side shoots.

SKIMMIA E S Occasionally remove some of the oldest wood and if necessary trim to shape in April.

SOLANUM E S/D/E CL Only a few species are sufficiently hardy for outdoor cultivation and most of these require wall protection. Some climbers are very vigorous and need drastic annual pruning in May when the previous year's shoots are cut back by half or even more, and all excess shoots are removed entirely.

SOPHORA E/D T/S The stronger kinds will make trees and should be trained to a central leader and feathered; the weaker kinds, whilst still trained to a central leader, are allowed to keep all side shoots or at the most these are only trimmed. After initial training there is no more pruning needed.

S. tetraptera is tender in its early years, for which reason it is often planted against a wall for protection. In the early stage young branches often interlace and at this stage no pruning is required, but when strong shoots grow out of the tangle some training is necessary. Once the tree has reached the top of the wall, it will be able to withstand a reasonable amount of cold and can be left to grow away naturally.

SORBARIA D S A strong grower with a suckering habit flowering on current season's growth. Prune back in March to within a few buds of well-developed framework.

SORBUS (mountain ash) D S/T The less vigorous kinds are allowed to develop several leaders, and pruning aims at keeping an open centre. Most kinds are trained to a single leader which is feathered; the smaller trees can be treated as standards. Once a framework has formed, it may be necessary occasionally to cut out a crossing branch. When trees carry large crops of berries which have escaped depredations by birds, the sheer weight of fruit can pull branches out of shape; pruning to correct this condition may be necessary in March. Most, if not all, species are susceptible to fireblight as well as to honey fungus.

SPARTIUM (Spanish broom) L S Its pithy stems tend to be soft and easily damaged if growing in shade or a rich soil. Trim shoots hard back to a framework in April.

SPIRAEA D S Some species flower on one-year wood, eg *S.* × *vanhouttei* and × *arguta*; these are cut back to where new growth is developing following flowering. Others such as *S.* × *bumalda*, *S. japonica* and *S. douglasii* flower on current season's growth and are pruned to within a few inches of ground-level during February.

STACHYURUS D S Occasionally remove some of the old wood, preferably in autumn.

STAPHYLEA D S Generally these have a suckering habit. During the winter remove some of the oldest wood, reducing the remainder and trimming to shape.

STEPHANANDRA D S Grown more for the graceful habit of stems and foliage rather than for flowers. During March remove some of the oldest stems carefully, trimming and thinning the remainder so as to retain the grace of habit.

STRANVAESIA E S Following training, thin out shoots in April if crowded.

STYRAX D S/T The strongest members should be trained to a single leader with all side shoots retained, but thinned if too crowded. The less vigorous kinds can be treated in the same way, or several leaders can be permitted. Prune in March, cutting out crowded branches and keeping the centres of bushes open. Trimming may be necessary in May if late frost causes damage.

SYCOPSIS E S During April, remove the dead and blind shoots from the centre of the bush, thinning and trimming to shape.

SYMPHORICARPOS D S All species have a suckering habit which can be invasive in a good soil; if so, clumps must be restricted. During March, remove the oldest and weakest shoots, thinning the remainder.

SYRINGA (lilac) D S/T If space is not limited, little pruning is required except for dead-heading and the removal of blind shoots from the centre of bushes. In small gardens there should be a reduction of some of the shoots and some trimming following dead-heading.

The stronger kinds will make small trees if trained and kept to a single leader; this needs regular attention because of the forking habit of lilac. Most cultivars of lilac are grafted either on to privet or wild lilac; suckers from the former stock are easy to recognize but those of the latter are not, therefore any shoot which emerges from beneath ground-level should be removed at the point of origin.

TAMARIX D S/T Some flower on one-year-old wood and these should be pruned following flowering, the wood which has flowered being removed and the resulting growths thinned. Others flower in late summer or autumn and these are pruned hard in March, being cut back to a framework; some thinning of resulting growth is desirable. The strongest kinds can be trained into small trees by selecting a central leader and reducing side shoots.

TAXODIUM (swamp cypress) D C Select and retain a central leader as long as possible. At maturity the natural habit is to produce a number of upright growths which are allowed to remain.

TAXUS (yew) E C Mostly these are trees but there are shrubby species and many kinds of the common yew *T. baccata* are shrub-like. Trees are trained to a central leader with all side branches retained though they can be reduced. Bush forms can be similarly trained or several leaders can be permitted. Some trimming to shape in April of these kinds may be necessary, when the centre of the bush should be cleared of clutter.

Irish yews can be trained to a single leader but the resulting tree may be too slender and require staking. Often several leaders are allowed but with age these tend to fall apart and some unobtrusive tying together of main stems is necessary to retain shape.

TEUCRIUM (germander) E S Some species are tender and need protection. All tend to sprawl and are untidy growers. In April cut back to shape and keep within bounds.

THUJA E C Select and retain a single leader, keeping all side branches; some trimming to shape may be necessary in April. Dwarf or small-growing forms are left unpruned.

THUJOPSIS E C Often rather untidy shrubs with several leaders which need some trimming in April.

THYMUS E S The mat types may need occasional attention to remove dead wood but if this becomes excessive the entire planting should be lifted and renewed. Those forming shrubs, eg the common Thyme *T. vulgaris*, are pruned in April when there is a thinning of shoots and most of the previous year's growth is trimmed back.

TILIA (linden or lime) D T Strong growers requiring plenty of room. Select a single leader and feather, training a well-spaced and balanced crown. When mature some species produce a rather dense crown and rather more drastic thinning than usual may be required here. Most species tend to produce masses of shoots along the length of their trunks. These should be removed by rubbing off while still soft.

TRACHELOSPERMUM E CL Most are slightly tender. Some have twining stems and some have roots that attach themselves to their supports. All produce masses of shoots, which if left become an unmanageable tangle. Drastically thin in May keeping only enough shoots to clothe the wall.

TSUGA E C Select and retain a single leader.

ULEX (gorse) L S Spiny shrub of dense habit which produces a lot of dead wood which if left becomes a fire hazard. Prune after the spring flowering, trimming back growth which has flowered and opening up the centre and removing dead wood. Trim after later flushes of flowering to prevent formation of seed.

ULMUS (elms) D T Select a single leader and feather, well spacing out the main limbs. Elms have a disconcerting habit of dropping large limbs without warning, so discourage undue extension of main branches. Dutch elm disease has become widespread in recent years and in spite of claims of resistance all species seem to be susceptible. Dead branches within a crown and premature yel-lowing are signs of trouble, and if the bark lifted on suspect branches discloses beetle galleries (the disease is spread by elm bark beetle) this confirms the disease. Heavily infected trees must be removed and such an operation is best left to qualified operators. Trees lightly infected will respond to lopping of infected branches if these are immediately removed and burnt. Check remaining branches to ensure that there are no beetle galleries.

VACCINIUM E/D S Occasionally some thinning may be required and trimming to shape. This is best done in early spring.

VIBURNUM D/E S A few species are tender and need wall protection. Some of the winter flowerers also need protection for their flowers. Little pruning is necessary but occasionally some of the oldest wood is removed and it may be desirable to trim to shape following a heavy fruit set. Winter flowerers are pruned in April or May; summer flowerers are cut in February or March, and evergreens are trimmed in April.

VITEX D S/T *V. angus-castus* flowers late in Britain when its blooms can be damaged by early frosts. It is therefore usually planted against a south or west wall where reflected heat helps to ripen wood, induce earlier flowering and provides blooms with protection against frost. Flowering is on current season's growth and in April all shoots are pruned hard back to a framework.

VITIS D CL If growing over a tree, no pruning is required. If on a wall, fence or pergola where space is limited, after training in several rods all side shoots are cut back to one or two buds of these in the winter. Do not delay pruning otherwise bleeding will occur.

WISTERIA D CL/S A very popular and beautiful climber that is too often planted where there is insufficient space or where no attention is given to pruning. All species are vigorous and if left to their own devices their long trails can dislodge slates, gutter and down pipes. Following planting, cut back stems by half, and continue to do this each spring until a well-spaced framework has been trained in.

87

In July all young shoots are cut back to four or five buds, and in February any further shoots which may have developed are cut back to two or three buds. This builds up a spur system and reduces extension growth, so encouraging the greatest number of flowers. If trained over a tree no pruning is necessary.

A free-standing shrub can be produced from a wisteria. Train in five leaders, cutting back to 90cm (3ft) in the first winter; the next winter cut the new extension growth back to no more than 90cm (3ft). Some support will be necessary and can be provided by attaching the framework, maypole-fashion, to a central leader. Prune all side shoots, as already described, in July and February.

ZELKOVA D S/T Select and retain a central leader for as long as possible. Reduce the number of side shoots but keep those which are retained for as long as possible.

ZENOBIA D S These shrubs have a suckering habit. Occasionally remove some of the oldest wood, tipping shoots in March. Dead-head and at the same time cut back to where new growth is breaking.

THE PRUNING OF FRUIT TREES AND BUSHES

8 Apples and Pears

The building of a fruit production unit

The principles and practice of pruning are put to the test with tree fruits more than with flowering shrubs or hedges. The latter need to be restrained and shaped but a few ill-considered cuts—or even pruning skipped for a year—will not result in lasting harm. The fruit tree is less amenable to the casual approach. To persuade it to produce regular crops from an early age it must be 'built' into a fruit production unit—often of unnatural shape—and every piece of growth must be assessed for its ability to increase fruiting potential.

This begins with the tree in the fruit nursery. Trees of the major British fruits are not grown on their own roots. The nurseryman has a choice of rootstocks which gives a range of tree sizes but with a small garden it is worthwhile to limit the vigour of the variety and encourage it to crop at an early date. Thus an apple variety (the scion) is budded or grafted on to a semi-dwarfing or dwarfing root (the stock) of the same family to produce a tree that remains 'bush' size. The gardener is advised to specify a bush tree when ordering apples or pears. Clearly there is no point in having a tall, vigorous tree that requires a ladder for pruning and picking in a small garden.

The year after budding or grafting, the scion bud sends up a single shoot and this first-year tree is known as a 'maiden'. These can be purchased by the gardener who wishes to carry out the critical first phase of training which is to secure the basic framework of branches. Alternatively this is done by the nurseryman, and the gardener buys a two- or three-year-old tree at a correspondingly increased price.

Before detailing the pruning procedure it is important to appreciate why a tree must be carefully 'built' from infancy. The bush tree is a good fruit producing unit which should have branches radiating around the trunk at a roughly equal distance apart. These branches should emerge from the trunk as close to the horizontal as possible—that is, approaching an angle of 90° with the trunk. Throughout its development, light and air must have direct access to all parts of the tree, particularly the centre, so that all the fruit develops full colour. A dense tree or one that is allowed to shoot up in columnar fashion is not efficient in the above respects; narrow-angle branches are more likely to split away under the weight of a heavy crop, and conditions in the dense centre favour the development of pests and diseases.

The continuing aim of fruit tree pruning— especially of apples and pears—is to keep the tree balanced in shape, and balanced in the proportions of old and young wood. 'Cutting back' is too simple a definition of pruning to apply to tree fruits. Such an arbitrary approach will only serve to delay and reduce the yield of fruit. An unpruned tree, if it is on dwarfing stock, will fruit early in its life and keep bearing. But—and this is why we prune—it will soon become crowded with growths, unhealthy, and bear small (if numerous) fruits irregularly.

So the gardener seeks a compromise by building a tree of manageable shape in the early years, and thereafter by selective pruning

Fig. 8.1. Winter pruning of young trees. (a) Newly planted 'maiden'; (b) Cut back to 60cm (24in); (c) The next winter before pruning; (d) After pruning: the new shoots selected as leaders have been cut back by two-thirds; (e) The following winter: the three-year-old tree before pruning; (f) After pruning: the leading shoots have been cut back again by about two-thirds; laterals to about three buds

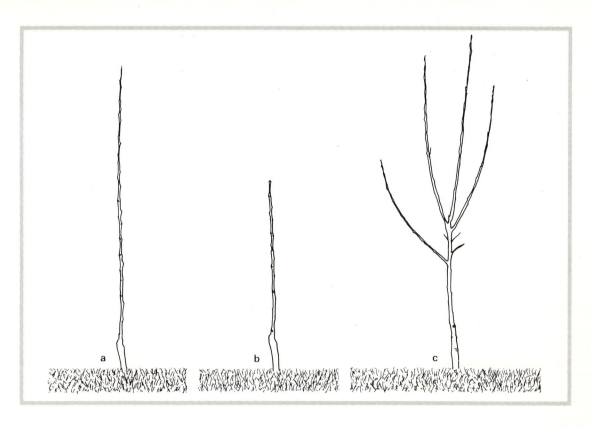

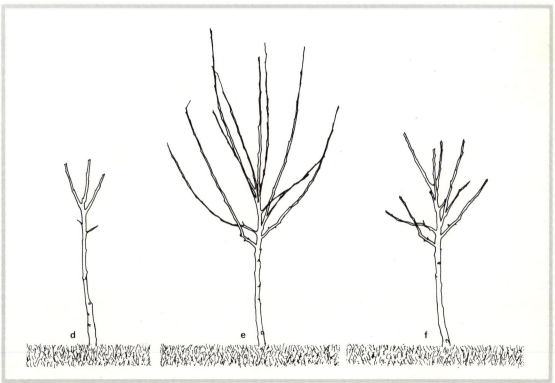

maintaining the same proportions while it grows bigger.

An important qualification is that different varieties have different natural growth habits which have to be taken into account in pruning. The soil also has an effect on tree vigour and the reaction to pruning.

Winter pruning of apples and pears can be tackled after leaf-fall and is better done early in the winter than late. Similarly a young tree is best planted and pruned in early winter. Summer pruning is the main method of pruning for trees grown in a restricted form. This helps to control vigour and exposes ripening fruit to sunlight if it is carried out in late July or early August.

We have seen that a tree may be purchased as a 'maiden' or as a two- or three-year-old. The maiden comes as a single shoot which must be cut back after planting. A bush tree is the only sensible shape for the modern garden and this means cutting back to leave a stem of about 60cm (2ft), using a sharp pocket knife or equally sharp secateurs (Fig. 8.1). From below this cut in the following spring the growth buds will produce shoots, the strongest just below the cut, the others in descending order of vigour. The top three shoots are retained as prospective branches of the tree. Ideally these branches should emerge at a wide angle from the stem, but the topmost bud always emerges at a narrow angle and grows up almost vertically. However the next bud down makes a better angle, so a way has been devised of treating the top bud so that it influences buds below it to grow out at a wide angle without making much growth itself. Before the buds break a small piece of wood is nicked out just below the top bud, so diverting most of the sap energy to buds below. The following winter the stub above the new top shoot is cleanly cut away. If any of the three top buds is close to its neighbour it is best cut out and another lower one allowed to grow.

We have reached the stage at which three shoots—framework branches—have been secured, either in the nursery before purchase or by the gardener. In the winter following their extension each of the three is cut back by about two-thirds. If possible prune to just above an outward-facing bud and always cut at a slight slope away from the bud.

From below this cut at least two shoots can be expected to extend from each parent branch. So the following winter there are six or more branches (six is a good number), which this time are cut back by half their length. One more year's development gives an 'adult' tree with an optimum of twelve branches spaced evenly all round. As its name implies, this is an open centre tree, with branches being produced over a short length of stem. The centre of the tree is not, however, completely open, having lateral shoots growing into it.

The aim of subsequent pruning

After this, hard pruning ceases and attention is directed towards keeping a balance between old and young wood. It is important to recognize by looking at the winter buds whether they will make growth shoots or flowers and fruit. Growth buds are slim and pressed tightly to the stem, while fruit buds are fatter and stand more away from the stem.

Look at a branch in winter that has been growing (and been pruned) for three years. The top section will be bearing mainly growth buds, the middle section mainly fruit buds, and the oldest section will have groups of fruit buds on small shoot systems called spurs. With the renewal pruning method this type of branch is allowed to crop for several years then replaced by a younger cropping unit. This will have been selected a year or two previous to its being used as a renewal shoot by having its leader cut back by about one-third.

As well as vigorous and potentially useful laterals from the main branches, short and weak growths will also appear. If these are well placed by having space around them and are not crowded, then they can be left full-length to form fruit buds. There still remain the vigorous laterals in the tree. Some should be retained as replacements (*see* above). Where they are badly placed, for example, competing with leading shoots, then they should be cut out completely and as close as possible to the branch which is to be left in.

This method of pruning tends to produce a tree with a good deal of growth in it. However, it is not as restrictive as older pruning methods and tends to the production of heavier crops starting from an early age. The weight of fruit on young shoots and branches brings them

Fig. 8.2. Summer pruning of a cordon apple. This is an essential part of the routine shaping of cordon trees. Note the shoot has gone 'woody', ie dark green to brown at the base before it is ready for pruning back to about five leaves

down nearer to the ground and this in turn encourages the production of further fruit buds. When these branches have been pulled down too far then they should be replaced.

Renewal pruning of apple trees

Some varieties of apple produce fruit buds at the tips of the shoots, eg Bramley's Seedling, Worcester Pearmain, Tydeman's Early. Account has to be taken of this when pruning and although, in the early years of tree formation, leader pruning leads to the removal of fruit bud, it must be continued until the basic tree shape has been established in these 'tip-bearing' varieties.

Pruning established trees

Provided trees are being fed regularly, trees should grow steadily after the formative years (say up to five years after planting). Leading shoots should not need to be shortened to keep them growing except in the case of replacement leaders. Vigorous and badly placed laterals should be cut out completely. Diseased, damaged, crossing and crowded shoots and branches should be removed. Large cuts need trimming up and painting with bituminous wound-protecting paint. With age, fruiting spurs formed from laterals become large and should be reduced in size.

Summer pruning, apples and pears

Summer pruning is carried out about a month before a variety is picked—say from mid-July to late August—and at such time there should be little if any regrowth from the cut shoots. Its result is to expose fruit and wood to the beneficial effect of light and air; it can reduce pest or disease incidence and will give a 'check' to vigour. Weakly growing trees should not be summer pruned. So shorten new shoots to 8cm (3in) or five leaves as they become woody at the base (Fig. 8.2). Trees grown in a restricted form, eg cordons, once established, should only be summer pruned. Bush trees can also be summer pruned and this will assist in controlling vigour.

Rejuvenating an old tree

Old apple and pear trees are often found in a neglected state, and fit at first sight only for grubbing out. However, with remedial pruning over a period of years such trees can be given a new lease of life. Neglect and abuse may have resulted in one of two ways. Where no pruning has taken place for years the tree will be overgrown with much branched fruiting spur systems with a lot of bare wood in them. The other possibility is that the tree has been 'hacked' instead of pruned so that it is a mass of congested shoots and quite fruitless.

In the first case, a procedure known as dehorning is adopted. Pears respond better to this than apples. It involves cutting out one or two branches each year as close to the crotch of the tree as possible. Initially remove branches that crowd the centre, and later thin out the periphery if necessary. Aim to reduce overall height by cutting to a point where a lower branch can take over. Cut cleanly at these junctions. If there are not many branches to be removed but spur clusters are crowded on old wood, thin out these clusters by half over a period of some four winters.

A tree that has been pruned so as to resemble a pollarded willow again needs whole branches cut out before shoot thinning is tackled on the remainder. Encourage a new framework of well-placed branches by selecting some of the best-placed shoots to be new leaders and tipping them. Leave enough of the others as laterals which will make fruit buds if left unpruned. In summer cut out at their base surplus 'watershoots' from old wood which will be produced in profusion unless pruning is spread over several seasons.

Pears

Fruit spurs form more easily and abundantly on pears than on apples, so that they are well suited to be trained in shapes, such as cordon or espalier. Bush trees can also be formed without any trouble, along the lines described for apples. With pears it is generally easier to achieve the ideal 'goblet' shape with an open centre.

To form a bush from a maiden tree, allow three well-spaced shoots to develop after cutting back to about 75cm (2½ft) above soil level as described for apples: then double the number by pruning each back by about one third. Then treat as described for apples but cutting back some laterals by about half to encourage more growth in the early years of the tree and counteract the tendency for vigour to decline as fruiting begins. Tip-bearing varieties, Joséphine de Malines and Jargonelle, need leader tipping until the framework of the tree is established.

Summer pruning is of more benefit to pears than apples, and is most important on trees trained to special shapes. The method is to reduce weaker side shoots to four leaves and stronger ones to six leaves in late July. This is followed by winter pruning back to two buds.

Leaders need to be cut back by a third in winter (with most apple varieties they are just tipped). Complicated spur clusters soon develop on pears and need to be thinned regularly to maintain fruit size.

Special tree shapes

Dwarf pyramid

By definition these trees are dwarf and pyramidal in shape. Dwarfness comes from the rootstock, and the best one for this form of tree under average soil conditions is called MM106: otherwise use M2 or MM111 where soil conditions tend to be unfavourable to growth. In contrast to an open-centred bush tree, the central leader must be retained to serve as the 'spinal column' of the pyramid. If a maiden is planted and then cut back in the normal way, the top buds must be stimulated into strong growth. The top one will be vigorous enough, but the next three or four can be encouraged by nicking out a small piece of bark above each one.

In the early winter of the following year these shoots are pruned back by half, cutting to a bud on the underside so that the shoots tend to grow out at a wide angle. Continue to winter prune the central leader so that it maintains vigorous vertical growth and keep the extension growth of the other main branches in proportion so that the shape continues to resemble a Christmas tree. As the leaders extend, tiers of side shoots will develop. Once the lowest side shoots have borne fruit all side shoots are summer pruned and spurred back in winter as described earlier for apples and pears. A pattern develops of tiers of laterals with sub-laterals.

Once the central leader has reached the maximum height desired, the relatively hard winter pruning of leaders ceases.

Cordon

This is a simple and rewarding way to grow apples and pears in a small garden.

As with other restricted tree forms, trees to be grown as cordons should be on a dwarfing rootstock and of an amenable variety. Cox's, James Grieve and Egremont Russet are suit-

able apples. The various cordon shapes and possibly dwarf pyramid trees require a supporting framework of posts and wire, which is best set up before the row is planted. Wires can also be fixed directly to a garden wall. There is little point in choosing a space-saving tree form unless several are planted, and this makes economical use of the posts and wire. These must be stout and durable, and wood posts—though the best looking—will need replacing eventually. Angle-iron or old piping is probably best and needs to be sunk deeply or buried in concrete. Concrete posts will also serve, though they tend to be bulky. Use strong wire and intermediate supports every 90cm (3ft) or so. Wires at 60, 90, 120 and 150cm (2, 3, 4 and 5ft) from the ground provide a good supporting system.

Best known of the variations on the cordon theme is the oblique cordon, and this is considered the best for the average garden.

The oblique cordon begins life as a single

Fig. 8.3. Single oblique cordons showing the supporting framework with shoots tied to bamboo canes. Note the flowers on short spurs along the lower parts of the cordons

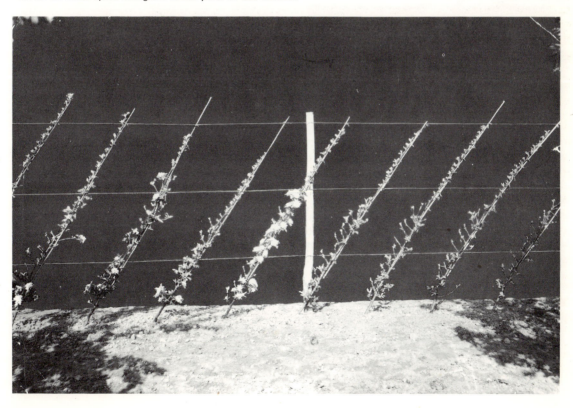

Fig. 8.4. Two fine fruiting upright cordon apples, showing the very heavy crops that can be obtained when apples are grown this way

bamboo cane is required, tied to the wire at a 45° angle, to which the maiden tree is secured with soft string.

The leading growth is allowed to extend each year, and cane and cordon can be lowered when the top wire is reached. This procedure reduces vigour and leads to plentiful fruit-bud formation. When the cordon has reached the limit of the space allotted to it, then the leading shoot should be treated like a lateral. Summer pruning is the main treatment for a cordon. It begins the summer after planting when shoots of the current year are shortened back to four or five leaves in late July/early August. In winter they are spurred back further. Thus spur systems develop in the lowest part of the stem and extend upwards each year. By the time most of the cordon is clothed with fruit spurs it is time to practise spur thinning on the oldest.

Use discretion in pruning according to tree vigour, cutting back thin weak shoots harder than average and very strong ones less hard. Cordon apples may also be grown in an upright form (Fig. 8.4).

Espalier

This horizontally spreading shape requires around 4·5m (15ft) of wall or post-and-wire space per tree. The system is built up in tiers, tapering to the top. A maiden is cut back to about 45cm (18in), to a bud above a pair lying opposite each other. The terminal bud and the two below are allowed to grow, the terminal being tied to a vertical cane on the wire-supporting framework, the two opposite shoots to cane at an angle of about 45° from the leader in order not to weaken them by making them horizontal at once (Fig. 3.1). They are lowered to the bottom wire at the end of the first growing season, but if one is weaker it is only partially lowered. The vertical leader is winter pruned back to about 60cm (2ft).

stem and remains thus throughout its cropping life. To form such a cordon of your own, start with a maiden tree and plant it close to the wire at an angle of 45° to the ground (Fig. 8.3). Allow 90cm (3ft) between each tree and plant so that the graft union (visible as a swelling just above the soil mark on the stem) faces the ground. This is done because the base of the tree will be under pressure and the union might split if facing upwards. With each cordon a

Above: Forsythia flowers on wood of the previous season's growth. To ensure an abundance of this type of growth it should be pruned hard immediately after flowering.

Above: Training pruning of young feathered trees. The first picture shows the removal of the lower branches, the second picture the shortening of the laterals to encourage the stem to thicken, and the third picture the removal of a developing double-leader.

Below: Cordon apples. The pictures show the training pruning of young maiden cordons. The third picture a row of well-trained established cordons.

Above top: *Salix alba,* one of the most spectacular of the willows grown for their winter bark, shown in the first picture. To achieve this, the plant needs to be pruned really hard each spring (second picture).

Above: Removing a double leader. If a double leader is allowed to develop, sooner or later the crutch will collect water, rot and the tree literally split itself down the middle.

Below: Summer pruning a pear tree. This operation is fully described in the text.

9 Plums and Cherries

Pruning risks for plums

Plum pruning is not without risk—to the tree. The spores of silver leaf fungus disease may gain entry through pruning cuts, and this disease is capable of killing a tree. What pruning is necessary should be carried out at the time of year the cuts heal rapidly and silver leaf infection is least likely. As the name implies, leaves on affected branches take on a silver appearance by comparison with healthy leaves.

Suspect the disease if you see much dead wood in a plum tree. If towards the end of the year, small bracket shaped fungi are produced on the dead wood it is almost certain that silver leaf is the cause. For confirmation, cut into suspected wood and look for a dark ring staining the wood; this is a sure sign that the fungus is present.

First action with an established plum or gage tree in the garden is to cut all dead branches back to healthy wood, preferably by mid-July, certainly before the end of August. If they prove to be silver leaf infected, cut back until no stain can be seen in the wood. Then paint the cut surfaces with a bituminous wound-protecting compound, and burn the prunings immediately.

Because of the risk of introducing this disease, all bush, half-standard or standard plum trees should be pruned as little as possible and, once the tree framework is established, only in summer. All that is required is to remove crossing branches that may rub together and any others that may be crowding the centre of the tree. Some varieties, such as Warwickshire Drooper, have a pendulous habit and the tips of a few branches may have to be cut back. Plums fruit on wood produced in the previous year and on spurs on older branches. If pruning in June or July means the removal of branches bearing unripe plums, the operation can be delayed until immediately after picking.

Plums are particularly prone to branch splitting, especially if the crop is heavy, and it is wise to have some props handy to support laden branches in a good year. However, if the worst happens, remove the broken branch immediately after fruit picking and cover all damaged surfaces with wound paint.

Establishment of a bush plum

In the average garden a bush plum, with 60–90cm (2–3ft) of trunk before the branches begin, is the best shape. Half-standards (Fig. 9.1), with a 1·2m (4ft) trunk, are useful for the more spreading varieties such as the popular Victoria. Plums are not suitable for growing in restricted forms such as cordon or espalier.

Nurserymen will supply one-year-old trees (maidens) or older trees on which a framework of branches has already been formed. If a two- to three-year-old tree is purchased, no pruning will be required until the spring a year after planting. To produce a bush tree from a maiden, the stem must be cut back to just above a bud, about 23cm (9in) above the desired position of the lowest branch. This is done after planting, in the spring and before bud burst. Small shoots low on the stem can be left, as they help to build up the tree until a number of strong branches have been formed. In July shorten the small shoots back to four or five leaves, and after two to three years remove them completely.

Pruning in the second year involves the selection of the main branches. A number of

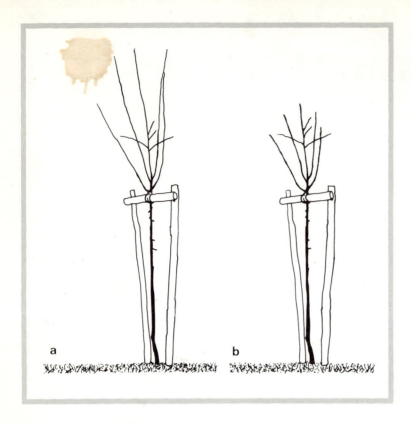

Fig. 9.1(a). Two-year-old half-standard tree before pruning, carried out just before growth starts in the spring; (b) The same tree after pruning. The shoots that are to form the main branches are cut back by half

strong shoots should have formed near the head of the tree, and about four of similar strength and evenly spaced round the stem are selected. These young branches ideally should make an angle as near as possible to 90° with the main stem. Such branches will be able to support a heavy weight of fruit, while those emerging at a narrower angle will be weak and prone to split. The chosen wide-angled branches are cut back in spring to a bud about halfway along their length while the remainder which form narrow angles and are badly placed are removed entirely.

In the third year, leaders (strong-growing branches) are cut back by half the growth they made in the previous year, and crossing and crowded shoots are removed. In subsequent years pruning is carried out in June or July and only involves the removal of dead, broken, crossing and crowded shoots as already mentioned.

Fan training for plums and gages

A possible training shape for plums and gages where a large area of wall is available is a fan.

Early training is similar to that for peaches, and is dealt with in that section (page 103). But once the framework has been built up and wall space filled, plums are treated differently because they fruit on both old and new wood. All pruning is carried out in the growing season and starts with rubbing out shoots that grow directly towards or away from the wall. Strong-growing upright shoots should be removed when young. Extension growths that are most suitable to fill a gap or replace an old branch are those on the lower side of older branches; these should be tied horizontally. This reduces their vigour.

Other shoots that are not wanted as leaders should be cut or pinched back in July to five leaves from their base, and are further shortened to a stub a few inches long as soon as the fruit has been picked. At the same time dead wood is removed, and naturally short spurs are left unpruned.

Plums are naturally vigorous and if fan-trained trees grow strongly without cropping, then root pruning will be necessary. This work is carried out in early winter (November–December) and involves digging a semi-circular trench round the tree about 75–90cm (30–36in) from the wall. Make the trench just over a spade's width and about 45cm (18in) deep. Remove all strong roots that cross the trench, chopping through them with the spade at each side of the trench. When the work is finished the soil is replaced and trodden down in layers a few inches deep at a time. During digging take care not to sever fine feeding roots. If a free-standing plum tree is to be root pruned to check excessive vigour, tackle half the root area one winter, the other half-circle the following year. Root-pruned trees will need particular attention to watering if dry weather occurs in the seasons following treatment They may need to be watered or mulched to conserve water in the soil.

Bullaces and damsons

Bullaces, small 'wild' plums ripening in autumn, and damsons, close relatives which ripen from mid-September onwards, are treated in exactly the same way as plums. A good framework of branches is built up in the first few years, and in subsequent years dead and less fruitful old branches are removed, together with any shoots that are crowding the centre of the tree.

Both bullaces and damsons live to a great age (fifty years is not unusual) and a neglected old tree can be rejuvenated by cutting most of the main branches back to near the trunk so that new shoots are produced that can be built into a new framework of branches. Always leave at least one large branch to act as a 'sap drawer'. Spread the work over two years, dealing with half the tree at a time. Spring, just before the buds burst, is a good time to carry out this work, but use a sharp knife to trim ragged cut surfaces, then immediately cover with bituminous wound-protecting paint.

Cherries

There are two distinct types of cherry; the sweet or dessert kind, and the acid cherry, of which the Morello is best known. With neither of them is winter pruning carried out owing to the risk of silver leaf disease infection.

Sweet cherries

These are not suitable for the small garden because no dwarfing rootstock is available and consequently they grow into large trees. Picking of what fruit has been left by the birds is difficult from a tall tree, and to ensure cross pollination two different varieties have to be planted. A fan-trained tree is the only feasible shape, and this requires sufficient wall space for two trees spaced 5·4–7·3m (18–24ft) apart. Even so, root pruning may be necessary in order to check vigour. However, birds can be kept from the fruit by draping netting over the tree.

The tree is built up in the same way as the peach (see page 103). Sweet cherries are pruned as little as possible once the framework is formed. Cut side shoots (laterals) back to five or six leaves in July, then shorten these again to three or four leaves in September. Rub out shoots that appear on the wall side of the branches as soon as possible, while they are small. Branch tips (leaders) are not pruned until they reach the top of the wall when they are bent over and tied down for a year. This will weaken them and encourage new shoots to break so that the following September the leaders can be cut back to replacement laterals. Also in September dead wood is removed and strong vertical shoots cut out, or tied down horizontally (which will weaken them).

Acid cherries

Acid cherries (Fig. 9.2) are not as vigorous as the sweet kinds and bush- or fan-trained trees can be planted in the garden about 4·5m (15ft) apart. They are more or less self-fertile and a single tree will set a good crop. The framework of bush trees is built up in the same way as for plums. Acid cherries fruit mainly on wood produced in the previous year, so once the framework of the tree has been formed subsequent pruning is aimed at encouraging this wood.

These cherries will make fresh growth from dormant buds on old wood, so each year a few branches are cut back to two-year-old wood in the case of young trees (about four or five years old), and to three- and four-year-old wood in the case of older trees. Once the tree is established a few of the older branches are cut back each year to encourage a supply of young shoots: this refers to fan-trained trees, not bush

Fig. 9.2. Acid cherries can be fan-trained against a wall to give a heavy crop in a confined space

trees. This is best done in April after buds have burst. Diseased and dead wood is also removed, as well as inward and crossing branches to keep the head thinned out. Once again, paint large cuts with bituminous wound-protecting paint to prevent silver leaf infection.

Fan-shaped trees are built up in the same way as for peaches (page 103). Pruning is the same except that side shoots can be closer, 5–8cm (2–3in) apart. On an established fan each year cut out a proportion of old branches and replace them with young shoots.

10 Peaches

Peaches flower early and in the British Isles the blossom is frequently killed by frost, with consequent loss of fruit. To obtain some protection they are often grown trained in a fan-shape against a south- or west-facing wall. However, in a relatively frost-free situation free-standing trees can be grown with fair prospect of fruit.

Free-standing bushes

Training a free-standing bush is easy enough. When a one-year-old tree (a maiden) is planted, it is cut back in the following May to a suitable side shoot (lateral) 45–60cm (18–24in) from the ground. Side shoots lower down the stem are removed entirely. In the following year there will be further side shoots which will compose the framework of branches. Cut these back by about one-third to an outward-facing bud. Shoots growing into the centre of the tree are removed and dead tips are cut back to a live bud.

The aim is to have branches arranged as evenly as possible in a spiral round the main stem. In subsequent years what pruning is necessary is carried out in May. It is only necessary to tip-prune any shoots that have died back and to remove branches that are crossing others or crowding the centre of the tree. When old branches get pulled down to the ground by weight of fruit they are cut back in May to a strong-growing vertical lateral.

Fan-trained trees

Trees are planted 23cm (9in) away from a wall and the branches are tied to horizontal wires spaced about 15cm (6in) apart so that they radiate like the spokes of a wheel (Fig. 10.1a–d). After planting in February a maiden tree is cut back to 60cm (24in) from the ground. As soon as shoots start to extend, one is left at the top plus a pair 20–23cm (8–9in) above the ground and close together but on opposite sides of the stem. The other buds are rubbed out with the thumb. The two lower shoots are encouraged to grow along bamboo canes fixed to the wires and radiating out from the stem at an angle of 45°.

When the shoots are about 45cm (18in) long the main stem above them is carefully cut out. If one shoot tends to grow more strongly than the other it must be brought down to a more horizontal position, which will restrain it.

In the second winter the two shoots are tied down to an even more horizontal position and cut back to about 45cm (18in). In the second summer a shoot at the end of each branch is allowed to grow along a cane to continue the growth of the main branch. Two shoots on the upper side of each branch are also allowed to grow, plus one on the lower side of each branch, and these are also tied to canes fixed to the wires. All other buds are rubbed out as soon as they can be handled.

In the third winter each new shoot is cut back by about one-third to a growth bud, on the upper side of the shoot if possible. Growth buds can be recognized because they are slender, while fruit buds are fat. If in doubt always cut to a triple bud cluster as these invariably consist of two fruit buds and one growth bud.

If there is space for a large tree, the treatment carried out in the second summer can be repeated once more, but otherwise steps are taken to secure a crop. To this end, third-summer treatment involves allowing the bud at the end of each of the eight branches to grow on, tying them to canes or directly to the wires.

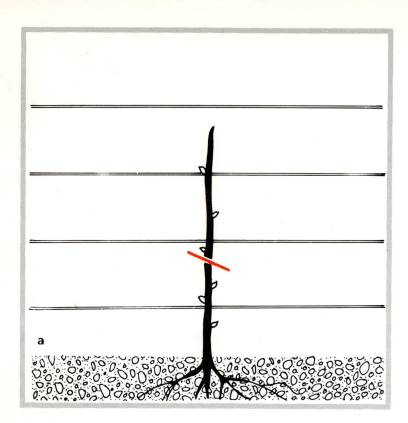

Fig. 10.1. (a) Maiden trees cut back to 60cm (2ft) at end of first winter

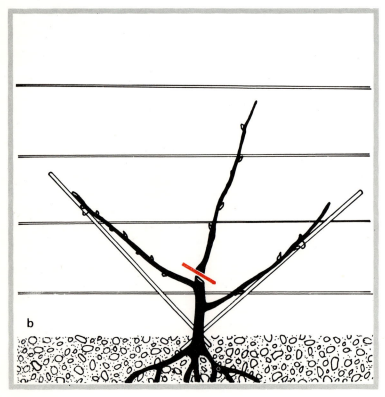

(b) Shoots selected to grow in required positions and the rest are rubbed out. Cut out the vertical shoot when shoots growing sideways reach 45cm (1½ft)

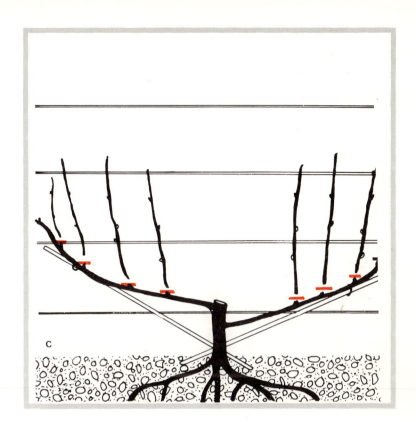

(c) Second winter: shoots are re-tied lower and cut back to 45cm (1½ft). Diagram also shows growth made in second summer and pruning cuts in third winter

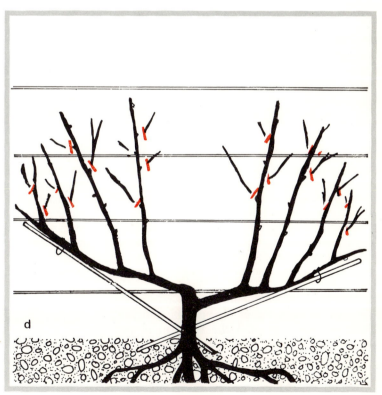

(d) third summer: new growth and subsequent pruning cuts

Fig. 10.2. Peach 'Princess of Wales', an old variety but still a good one, showing how a peach needs to be trained fairly flat against a wall to obtain maximum ripening of both wood and fruit

Rub out shoots that grow directly towards or away from the wall. Shoots from the remaining buds on both sides of the branch are kept where they can be spaced about 15cm (6in) apart, and excess buds are rubbed out.

Once the shoots have grown to about 45cm (18in) the tips are pinched out. They are tied to the wires so they are spaced 10–15cm (4–6in) apart. These shoots should bear fruit the following year.

Fourth and subsequent summers require the removal of superfluous shoots, the pinching back of shoot tips and the tying-in of new shoots that will bear fruit in the following year. To obtain replacements for fruiting shoots, one shoot from a wood bud at the base is allowed to grow. Two shoots can be taken if there is a space to be filled. If the wall space is filled pinch new growths back to four leaves after six or seven have been formed.

Shoots close by a developing fruit are pinched back to two leaves. After the fruit has been gathered, fruit-bearing wood is cut off close to its replacement, which is then tied to the wires. Dead or diseased wood is removed at the same time. Fig. 10.2 shows the fruit production obtainable from a mature tree.

Nectarines

A nectarine is a peach without the soft hairs on the skin, and is pruned in exactly the same way. Being more tender than peaches, nectarines are not usually successful as outdoor bush trees.

Apricots

This fruit likes a warm climate and flowers even earlier than the peach so that in Britain frosts often kill the blossom outdoors. For this reason apricots are generally grown in a fan-shape against a warm wall and covered with a few layers of fine mesh netting when frost threatens. It is even worth erecting a polythene screen round the tree when flowering starts in February. Hand pollination with a paint brush then becomes necessary. This is a good idea in any case with apricots, which are self-fertile.

Pruning follows the same pattern as for peaches, but as flowers are produced on spurs on older wood as well as on the previous season's shoots, spurs are encouraged by pinching back laterals when they are about 8cm (3in) long.

On rich soils apricots are prone to produce excessively long shoots but few fruits. If this happens, vigour can be checked by lifting and replanting the tree if it is small enough, or by root pruning (page 139) if it is large.

11 Vines

It is easy to regard grapes as an exotic crop for the greenhouse, and to some extent this is true if large dessert berries are desired. But in many parts of the country, particularly in the south, a good crop can be obtained outdoors. If the right varieties are chosen these are usually excellent for wine-making and, in exceptional seasons, for eating as well.

Vines under glass

The easiest method is to train vines as single cordons, that is with a permanent single stem called a rod, from which side shoots grow each year and bear the bunches of grapes. As the best grapes grow on a current year's shoot, arising from the stub of one pruned the previous year, the pruning method has this end in view, ie of keeping a succession of shoots forming from the stubs of the previous year's growth.

Young vines are usually planted just outside the greenhouse or conservatory and the main stem taken through a gap in the wall into the house. This is done to provide better conditions for the roots. If it is more convenient, the vine can be planted in the greenhouse but more watering will be required and this could be a problem during holidays.

A supporting system of horizontal wires is necessary (Fig. 11.1). They must be 23cm (9in) apart and at least 23cm (9in) below the glass to avoid leaf scorching. The vine is planted in winter and cut hard back. The following season the strongest young shoot is allowed to grow up towards the apex of the house and the others are rubbed out. This leader will produce laterals (side shoots) and these are pinched out at the tip when 45–60cm (18–24in) long. Sub-laterals (side shoots from the laterals) are pinched when they have produced one leaf. It

is important to space the laterals carefully so they are about 45cm (18in) apart on alternate sides of the main stem. Badly placed or additional laterals must be removed while they are young enough to be rubbed out.

The vine will be ready for its first annual pruning when the leaves change colour in autumn, just before they fall. Although the rod may have reached the top of the greenhouse in the first year, it should be cut back to a bud where the shoot is well ripened. Cut back the laterals on the rod to one or two buds in order to build up a spur system. The following year a leading shoot is allowed to continue extension growth until the roof area has been filled. Laterals are selected on alternate sides every 45cm (18in) and stopped as before. Once this main shoot has grown to its maximum extent it is treated as a lateral.

Returning to the laterals that were cut back to spurs the previous autumn, these will produce new shoots in spring which, when 2·5–5cm (1–2in) long, are reduced to two per spur by rubbing the rest out. If the lowest spurs are slow to produce new growths, untie the rod from its supports and arch it down close to the ground until growth can be seen: also spray the rod with warm water on sunny days.

As they grow, tie the selected laterals to the framework of wires. Flower trusses will soon start to form on them, and further growth is then pinched out at two to four leaves beyond the truss. Sub-laterals are stopped at one leaf. It is usually necessary to reduce the number of bunches so that remaining grapes will swell

Fig. 11.1. (a) Winter pruning: two shoots tied down to lower wire. Third shoot cut back to three buds
(b) August: fruiting laterals trained through double wires. Replacement shoots allowed to grow on

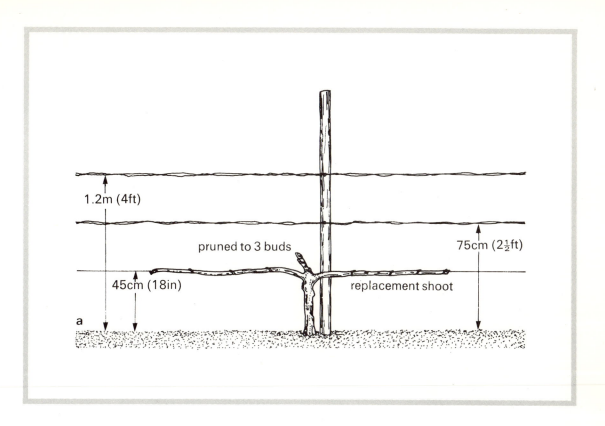

1.2m (4ft)

75cm (2½ft)

pruned to 3 buds

45cm (18in)

replacement shoot

a

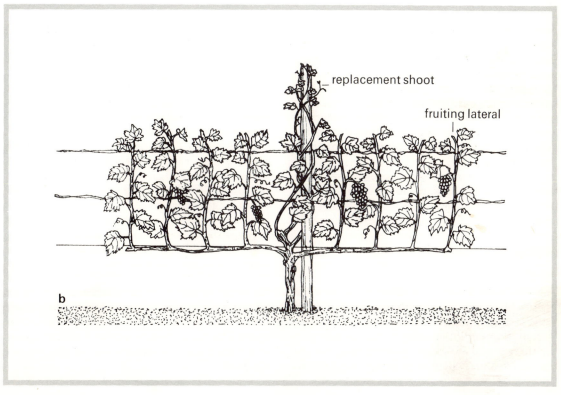

replacement shoot

fruiting lateral

b

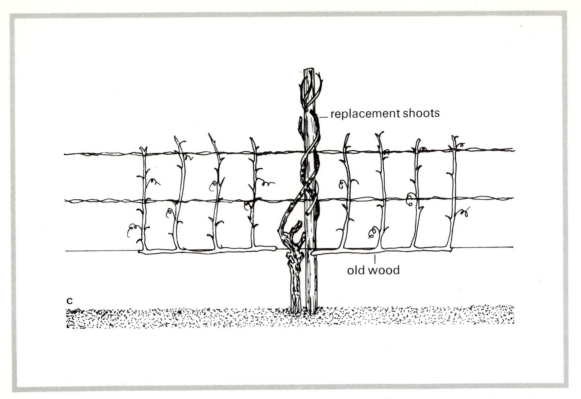

Fig. 11.1 (c). November: old wood cut out and three replacement shoots ready for training—two for tying in; one to left and one right

to a good size. Some bunches can be removed when the flowers are seen to have set, the remainder when the grapes have started to swell. As a guide, work to the formula of one bunch to 23cm (9in) of rod. So that each bunch is not overcrowded, cut out some of the berries with a fine-pointed pair of scissors. The remainder will be larger as a result. Of course, grapes for wine-making need not be thinned as much as those for the table.

The final job in the year's programme is to cut the laterals back to about two buds in autumn, leaving only short spurs along the main rod.

Vines outdoors

A south- or south-west-facing wall is an ideal place to grow a vine. A suitable shape is a fan tied to horizontal wires with two or three main rods carrying laterals. Training is the same as for vines under glass, except that initially two or three main shoots are allowed to grow. As before, a spur system is built up with laterals cut back close to the main rods in autumn.

The training method about to be described is suited to vines grown in rows—that is, without the support and protection of a wall—but the method can be adapted to wall training.

Vines supported in rows by wires can give good crops, especially in the south of England and if glass or polythene screens can be used to help ripening in late summer. The vines are planted 1·35m (4½ft) apart in a row running north–south or on a south-facing slope. Two wires are stretched along the row at 30cm (1ft) and 60cm (2ft) above the ground. Plants are set out during winter and cut hard back to encourage strong growths in summer. Three strong growths should be selected and they will probably have to be cut back again in the second winter until the plant is well established and growing strongly. In the third winter two of the three shoots are bent down and trained in opposite directions along the lower wire. They are pruned back to between five and seven buds. The third shoot is cut back to three buds to produce three strong shoots for the following year.

The two shoots that have been trained on the

bottom wire and tied down will produce laterals from each bud. These will grow up to the top wire, to which they are tied. When the bunches of blossoms are opening (about June) the fruiting laterals are stopped a few centimetres above the top wire by going down the row with shears.

If berry size is important, the bunches can be thinned when the grapes are swelling, leaving the best bunch on each lateral. Trimming with shears may be needed at intervals during the season to keep growth in check, and unwanted growths along the main stem and laterals should be rubbed out while small. The three replacement shoots are allowed to grow without stopping.

Glass or plastic panels along each side of the row in late summer will help ripening, but leave the top open for growth to come up and be trimmed back at intervals.

Pruning takes place once again after leaf-fall when the two fruiting arms are untied from the lower wire and cut away close to the main stem, while two of the replacement canes are tied down in opposite directions to the lower wire and shortened as described above. Again, the third shoot is cut back to three buds to form the replacement shoots.

Vines can also be grown under large barn cloches, and pruning is largely the same except that only two new shoots are required each year. One wire only is needed, 23cm (9in) above the ground. One shoot is shortened to eight buds and tied to the wire, while the other is cut back to two buds. These two buds will produce the replacement shoots. Cloches are put over the row in summer. Grapes are produced on the laterals that grow from the shoots tied to the wire. Stop these laterals at two leaves beyond the bunches.

12 Currants and Berries

Blackcurrant

Blackcurrant is an easy-to-grow and valuable bush fruit: valuable because it is one of the richest sources of vitamin C, while ease of culture includes pruning. It also extends to propagating so that there is no excuse for keeping old and unfruitful bushes in the garden. Ten years is a good life for a blackcurrant bush, by which time cropping is likely to be much reduced by 'reversion' virus, spread by a microscopic mite Blackcurrant Gall Mite. Mites breed within blackcurrant buds which appear abnormally big, giving rise to the condition called 'big bud'.

It is important to plant only healthy bushes, such as those certified by the Ministry of Agriculture and then to take precautions against Gall Mite by spraying with Lime Sulphur. Once big buds appear on bushes, however, then reversion is almost certain to follow and pruning out affected shoots will not prevent the whole bush from becoming reverted in time. Such bushes should be grubbed out and burnt at the first sign of reversion.

Growth and roots are produced prolifically by this fruit, and it is the gardener's job to promote those buds best placed to rejuvenate the bush. It follows that basal growth gives maximum renewal, and roots that develop on basal suckers are beneficial. Avoid at all costs the formation of a leg or stem on blackcurrant bushes. Foundations for a good shape are laid when the young bush is first planted by cutting the existing shoots back to 2·5 cm (1 in) above the soil, *see* colour plate. Buds will break below these cuts and send up a cluster of shoots. In the autumn of the same year cut back any of these young shoots close to soil-level which have not reached a length of 30 cm (12 in).

Those remaining should be left full-length and will bear fruit the following summer. They will also give rise to side shoots destined to fruit the year after, along with the regrowth from the cut-back shoots. In autumn again it is time to prune out a proportion of the shoots that have carried fruit. A reliable rule of thumb in pruning established bushes is to remove—by cutting out close to the soil—a quarter of the *old* wood each year. The old wood can be distinguished by its dark colour. Young shoots are light brown but as time passes they darken to an almost black colour with age.

It is tempting to make pruning cuts just above vigorous young growths that arise about halfway up the older wood. But if many cuts are made at this height the bush soon becomes tall, spindly and weakened as the supply of vigorous basal shoots dwindles. So be firm and cut low: there will be ample renewal each year to replace the top growth which has been removed. As well as old wood removal, encourage further suckering by cutting hard back the weakest of the new basal growths each autumn. Pruning to this pattern will give the ideal balance of older and younger shoots, especially if allied with generous manuring.

It is possible to prune blackcurrants after fruit picking and while still in leaf without apparent detriment. A more usual time for pruning, however, is during the winter, viz. November/February.

Suckering and rooting near the soil surface is the aim, and is encouraged by applying mulches of straw, peat or rotted compost over the root area in early summer to keep the soil cool and moist. By the same token it is unwise to cultivate around the bushes and risk severing roots. Remove weeds by hand if possible or hoe very superficially and with great care.

Red and white currants

Red and white currants are rarely seen in shops, which is good enough reason to grow them. In spite of their name they are quite unlike the blackcurrant in that they are grown on a single stem or leg, and in this respect they are much more like the gooseberry, which they also resemble in bearing fruit on spurs on the old wood and are, therefore, pruned in the same manner as gooseberry. When cuttings of these currants are prepared for rooting, the buds on the bottom 15cm (6in) of stem are rubbed out or cut away so they will not grow and the bush is left with a clean leg. This will have been carried out on bushes purchased by the gardener. It is sufficient to keep four well-spaced shoots initially at the top of the stem, and to cut these back by about half in the first winter. The following year a framework of about eight branches will be established and, again in winter, the leaders should be cut back by about half.

Unlike the blackcurrant which fruits only on wood made the previous year, the red and white currants keep making fruit buds on the old wood year after year, so that old wood cannot be cut away without sacrificing a substantial amount of potential fruit. Suckers can arise from ground-level but are best torn away at the point of emergence in order to maintain the clean leg referred to previously.

Many side shoots are also produced and currant bushes will rapidly become a forest of growths unless pruned in summer as well as winter. This is done in late June, shortening side shoots to within 8–10cm (3–4in) of the main branches.

Winter pruning consists of cutting the side shoots back further, to two buds or 1cm ($\frac{1}{2}$in). Winter pruning by about half of leading shoots should be continued for several years, but then can be harder as bushes fill the available space. From time to time cut out an old shoot and replace it by a new one.

Birds like to eat unprotected buds on these currant bushes in winter, as well as sampling the fruit in summer, so it is wise to grow them within a bird-proof fruit cage.

To summarize the pruning process: preserve a clean stem or leg; establish a vase-shaped structure of about eight main branches; shorten back all side shoots in summer and again in winter, and tip-prune leaders in winter. Allow for the occasional replacement of an older branch by a suitably placed younger one.

Red and white currants can be trained as cordon bushes to economize on space in the garden. Wires strained between posts are the ideal support. Set the bushes 30cm (1ft) apart sloping at an angle of 45° and tied to a bamboo cane which is itself attached to the wires. Allow only one branch to grow as the leader, which should be tip-pruned back by one-third of its annual extension growth each winter. Prune all side shoots to 10cm (4in) in summer, then cut back to 1cm ($\frac{1}{2}$in) in the winter. Fruit will form in a column on these spurs. When the desired height has been reached, leading shoots can be treated like laterals. Cordon currants are less attractive to birds because they do not provide a good 'footing'.

Gooseberry

Gloves are essential when tackling gooseberries with secateurs, and are also advisable at picking time. Garden bushes are grown on a clean stem or leg and, as with red currants, a semi-permanent framework of branches is established. However, the gooseberry fruits on both one- and two-year-old wood, so that removal of a proportion of old wood each year will not jeopardize fruiting (Fig. 12.1a–e).

If the bush is pruned on a replacement system rather like the blackcurrant, it is likely to fruit heavily but these fruits will tend to be small and most suitable for bottling. If, on the other hand, a spur-pruning system is adopted, such as was described for the red currant, there may be fewer fruits but they will be large and of dessert quality.

So, if size of berry is not important, winter-prune the bush by cutting out at low level the older central wood in order to open up the bush and make picking easier. New growth on the chosen leading branches should be cut back by a half. Pruning for quality involves summer pruning of all side shoots to 10–13cm (4–5in) followed in winter by 'spurring back' to 5cm (2in). From then on, regrowth from these spurs is cut hard back to its base. Limit the number of leader branches to a maximum of eight, and

Fig. 12.1. A sequence showing the pruning of a gooseberry bush. Regular, routine pruning leads to larger fruits and heavier crops. It also helps to control some pests and diseases

in winter cut back the annual extension growth by about half. Gooseberry varieties that have a drooping habit should be leader-pruned to counteract this tendency making the cuts on the leaders to an outward and upward pointing bud. As with red currants, birds will go for the buds in winter and it is best to keep gooseberries in a fruit cage. Failing this, some protection against birds should be given and pruning delayed until just before bud burst in spring, when cuts can be made close to those buds which have been left intact.

The great advantage of cordon training for the gooseberry (apart from being space-saving) is that picking is made so much easier. Training and pruning follows the pattern already presented for red and white currants. It makes good sense to grow both types of fruit on the same framework.

Raspberry

Autumn is the best time to plant new raspberry canes. Once planted they are pruned back to 30cm (1ft) from the ground, cutting just above a bud. The following year these canes will be developing their root systems and sending up new canes (spawn). It is these that bear the first crop of berries the following summer.

It is best to provide raspberries from the outset with supporting wires stretched between posts. The first flush of new canes the summer after planting should not be pruned, although weak ones are best removed. The original canes are cut out at ground-level that autumn.

Regular pruning and thinning out begin in the second summer. More new canes than are required are produced along the row, and weak ones should be pulled off when they can be distinguished. Make a point of removing those furthest from the parent canes in order to keep the row narrow and easily supported. As a rule of thumb, keep six at the most from the group that has sprung from the parent root.

Treatment of canes that have carried fruit is simplicity itself. Cut them all out at ground-level soon after picking, and burn them as a precaution against spread of disease. Then,

115

116

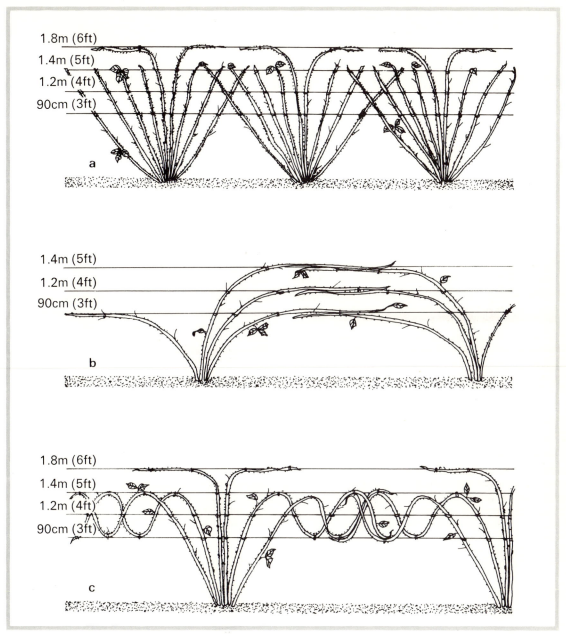

Fig. 12.2. Three different ways of training loganberries and blackberries, etc.: (a) fan; (b) rope; (c) weaving

having selected and retained the best of the new canes, these are tied securely but not tightly to the wires. A continuous looping run of soft string is a good way to secure them.

February is the time to tip-prune the new canes, removing the top 8cm (3in). This is done partly to remove damaged tips and partly to stimulate fruiting shoots below.

With the autumn-fruiting varieties such as 'September' fruit is borne on the current season's growth and new canes must be cut down to about 10cm (4in) above ground in February–March.

Loganberry

A loganberry is generally trained in a fan-shape against a wall, fence or post-and-wire framework. After autumn planting existing cane is cut back to 23cm (9in) above ground. Two or more new growths should arise at ground-level the following year. These are spaced and tied to horizontal wires with soft string (Fig. 12.2). The following year these canes will bear fruit. The main pruning operation consists of their complete removal after picking.

The loganberry grows vigorously and a disciplined approach to training is required to prevent it becoming unkempt. By the time the first fruit-bearing canes are cut away there will be a flush of new growths. The weakest can be removed at once and a maximum of eight strong ones tied on to the supporting framework fan-wise on either side. This can be done in autumn or delayed until spring on exposed sites. Secure the shoots so that the centre of the fan is left open to receive the following season's new growths. These in their turn will be lowered to re-form the fan when the older ones are cut out. This effectively separates old and young canes each year, and so young growths are less liable to be infected by any disease spores on the older parts.

In February the tips of the canes which are above the top wire (1·5–1·8m (5–6ft) high) are cut off. Growths that sprout an inconvenient distance from the parent root should be cut away at an early stage. These and blackberries are thorny subjects and gloves need to be worn during training and pruning operations. If you are planting for the first time take advantage of the thornless varieties of both fruit that are available and which are much easier to manage.

Blackberry

The pruning and training approach described for the loganberry can be applied to the blackberry—though this fruit is even more precocious in its annual growth and needs a firm hand to keep it within bounds. It bears fruit on the same wood for several years but it is best to cut out growths after they have fruited.

A similar method of training should be followed. New growth should be trained up to and along the top-most wire of the supporting framework each year. Old cane should be removed after it has fruited. In early spring the new growth should be untied and trained out over the lower wires to fruit, leaving the top-most wire free for new growth to be trained along it during the summer again.

Other hybrid berries

Certain hybrid berry fruits are offered by nurserymen, most of which are akin to the loganberry or blackberry, while others have currant *Ribes* in their 'blood'. Generally they are less hardy and less vigorous than their cousins. They may indeed be damaged by hard frost. Examples are the boysenberry, youngberry and veitchberry. The wineberry is attractive in growth but has fruits of poor eating quality. Maintain a balance of fruiting and replacement growth in all cases.

THE PRUNING OF HEDGES AND GREENHOUSE PLANTS

13 Hedges

A hedge can serve many purposes in a garden; as a boundary marker it may also offer protection against stock, shelter from wind, provide privacy or hide from view unsightly objects. Within, it can divide up a garden, form a screen, provide a background to plants or architecture, whilst in varying heights can be used as edgings to beds or paths.

Broadly there are two types of hedge; formal and informal. Formal hedges are trimmed regularly to retain sharp outlines; those which are informal are grown primarily for flowers and/or fruit and are trimmed just to keep within bounds. In either group it is usual but not essential to use the same plant for the entire hedge. In fact a pleasing feature can be made by making a mixed hedge of different kinds of flowering shrubs in an informal hedge (Fig. 13.1) or, in a formal hedge, by alternating say a green and a copper beech or planting together hollies with different colours of variegation.

Pay some attention to the kind of plant that will be used in the hedge. Choose a plant which is suited to your soil conditions; avoid acid-

Fig. 13.1. An informal hedge of mixed shrubs. Such hedges need only occasional pruning to keep within bounds

lovers on chalk, moisture-lovers on a dry soil or plants requiring good conditions on a soil that is poor. Selection of hedge plants can be governed by tolerance to salt in maritime districts or atmospheric pollution in towns and cities, whilst in country areas stock may be a problem. Rate of growth is important, for a plant which is rapid growing may quickly provide privacy but become too tall for easy maintenance and cut out much needed light whilst at the other extreme, something which is slow growing or of too low stature may take too long or never provide privacy. Finally, or perhaps it should be considered first of all, there is cost.

Hedges once planted will occupy ground for many years so thorough soil preparation before planting is essential. Mark out the line that the hedge is to occupy bearing in mind its eventual width. Double dig a strip of ground a metre (yard) wide and incorporate as much organic matter as possible in the lower spit. Allow to settle, tread and before planting remove surplus soil so that hedge plants will finish up in a shallow depression; this will make for easier watering. Hedges should never be planted on a raised bed unless the ground lies wet during the winter. Immediately prior to planting apply a dressing of a general fertilizer at the rate of 68g/m (2oz/yd) of row and rake in. Deciduous subjects can be planted at any time from leaf-fall until growth recommences, whilst evergreens and conifers go in in mid-April. Buy young plants, one or two years old which though small are cheaper, will establish readily and grow away more quickly so passing larger, older and more expensive specimens. Many nurseries offer hedging plants at a favourable rate of so much per hundred.

A hedge should be planted in a single line with plants well spaced at between 60–90cm (2–3ft).

Training pruning

Deciduous shrubs are cut back in March following planting by one half so as to ensure branching from near ground-level; the aim with any hedge is to produce and maintain a well-furnished base. In the following winter upright new growth is reduced by one third to one half and all side shoots are trimmed back by a half. The third winter again the upright growth is reduced by a third and all side shoots trimmed back by the same amount. Evergreens are trimmed in April following planting just before new growth begins. The leading shoots are left untrimmed with all the side shoots reduced by a third. This treatment is repeated in the following two years. Conifers are left unpruned. If, however, conifers or evergreens are bare at the base when bought, the rules formulated will have to be broken and leading shoots cut back by a third to encourage growth to break from low down.

This initial pruning is the same for formal or informal, deciduous or evergreen subjects. During this training the hedge will be developing naturally with a broader base tapering to a narrower top (Fig. 13.2).

During these growing seasons and in subsequent ones, keep the hoe moving along the base of the hedge to keep down annual weeds, carefully forking out any perennials before they become established. Include the hedge with roses, fruit or general garden in routine spraying so as to control aphids and caterpillars. Water in dry spells at least until the hedge is established. Each March give an annual dressing of a general fertilizer at 68g/m (2oz/yd) to each side of the hedge. In the early years a mulch over the area of soil on each side that the roots occupy will be beneficial. Remove any material resulting from clipping or pruning and take right away. Always keep the hedge bottom free from rubbish as this provides hiding places for pests.

Established pruning

Informal hedges
There will be one pruning a year and its timing will depend on the age of wood on which flowers are produced. Those which flower on current season's growth are trimmed to shape whilst dormant, between January and March. Others, flowering on previous season's growth, will be trimmed to shape after flowering. During this pruning there will be a removal of old flowering wood and a thinning of overcrowded or weak growth.

Formal hedges
Usually there is only one pruning necessary for deciduous subjects and this is carried out

Fig. 13.2. Three examples of
training hedges into formal
shapes:
(a) Loaf shaped

(b) Elongated pyramids

Above: Black currant. These can be severely pruned as shown here. When cut to ground level they will produce plenty of young shoots, but will not usually fruit well until the second year after this type of pruning.

Below: Raspberry canes tied in after pruning.

Above: A well-kept hedge is a joy in any garden. Modern powered hedge-trimmers now considerably reduce the effort in keeping a hedge neatly trimmed.

Below: Pruning evergreens. Most evergreens should be pruned in May. Care should be taken not to cut the leaves, as they will brown where cut.

Below right: Spur-thinning a pear tree.

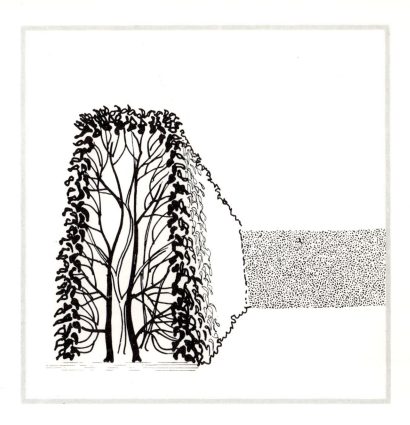

(c) Oblong

during the winter when shrubs are dormant. Sometimes there is additional trimming of growth during the growing season. Evergreens are trimmed in August when new growth has finished and wood is beginning to ripen. Most of the new growth is removed in the clipping. Conifers are allowed to grow naturally until they have grown together to form a screen. Upward development is only stopped when the desired height has been reached but when leaders are beheaded there is a tendency for the hedge to thicken. When this stage has been reached, trim the sides of the hedge in August when most of the current season's growth is removed.

In the initial training, secateurs are the best tools to use and should continue to be used on hedges composed of large-leaf subjects as well as for most kinds of informal hedge. Shears or power cutters can replace secateurs for formal hedges of small-leaf subjects and can be used on informal or semi-informal hedges if these also have small leaves, eg *Berberis × stenophylla*. A formal hedge with a long straight face needs careful cutting to produce an even surface for any carelessness in cutting on such

a sweep will be immediately noticeable. Always use shears or power cutters with their cutting edges flat against the surface; do not poke their tips into the hedge (Fig. 13.3). Continue to keep a broad base with a narrow top to ensure a well-furnished base. With practice, a gardener will develop a good eye and may well be able to cut without any aids. For the less experienced, a broad piece of wood with length equivalent to height of the face of the hedge can be laid against the sloping surface for guidance. To ensure that the top is cut level, drive two stakes of equal height into the hedge and stretch a line tightly between the two (Fig. 13.4). It is important that there is no sag in the line otherwise the top will not be even.

Edging

Edging is the use of low-growing shrubs to produce a hedge in miniature usually less than 60cm (2ft) in height in exactly the same way as for a formal hedge. Such edges around beds were popular in earlier centuries: in knots of the 16th and parterres in the 17th. At that period within living edges, beds could be filled

125

Fig. 13.3. The blades of shears (or power cutter) should be laid flat against a hedge when it is being trimmed

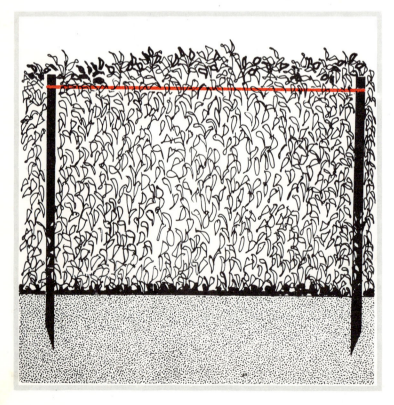

Fig. 13.4. Stretching a line in order to obtain a straight level line across the top of a hedge

126

with coloured earths, sands, gravels or pebbles or they might contain low-growing evergreen shrubs which, like the edges, were kept clipped. Such beds were essential in the age of the great formal gardens and the sharp lines had to be maintained to ensure that there was a sharp geometric symmetry. Today, edging of beds is much less common but it can be seen in use around beds in a rose or herb garden and for use along the front of a herbaceous border or to mark the edge of a pathway.

As for a hedge, thoroughly prepare the soil. Double dig the entire bed or border, not just the strip that the edging will occupy, working in as much organic matter as possible into the second spit. Allow to settle, tread and apply a dressing of a general fertilizer at the rate of 68g/ sq m (2oz/sq yd) and rake over the soil of the entire bed or border. Plant in April either in a single or staggered double row depending on the eventual width required. If the bed or border is also to be planted in the same year, ensure that the outside row is well away from the edging. Once the edging is established, planting within the bed can come much nearer the edge.

Following planting the edging is lightly trimmed over on top and along the sides. In subsequent years this trimming is continued in August with a second trimming taking place as new growth is about to start in April. Additional summer clippings can be carried out during the growing season to ensure that lines are sharp. Until the desired skill has been acquired, cut on the light side so that a second cut is always possible to allow correction of a fault. It is very difficult to be able to rectify a mistake following a hard clipping. Keep weeds away from the base for if these once establish they are extremely difficult to remove. In the early years watering may be desirable until the plants are well established. If manure or compost is being dug into the bed or border work some in close to the edging. An annual feeding of the edging should take place in early April at the rate of 68g/m (2oz/yd) of hedge, scattering over a strip of 60–90cm (2–3ft) wide. Some plants suitable for using as edging plants are: common thyme, lavender cotton, lavender, dwarf box and germander.

In the following list suitable subjects are cited for making formal or informal hedges, also included are those that can be used for edging. From the details given it should be possible to find a subject which is suitable for your own conditions.

Abbreviations

D	deciduous	F	formal
E	evergreen	I	informal

ACER CAMPESTRE (hedge maple)
D F/I 3·6m (12ft) Trim in winter. Suitable for growing on chalk; golden autumn colour.

AUCUBA JAPONICA
E F/I 1·8m (6ft) Trim in August with secateurs. There are several cultivars with different patterns of variegation. Suitable for a wide range of soils; tolerant of shade and pollution. Female plants in the presence of males will produce red berries.

BERBERIS DARWINII
E F/I 2·4m (8ft) Trim after flowering. Suitable for most soils; tolerant of pollution and salt. Produces orange flowers in spring and erratically throughout the year, to be followed by blue-black fruits (Fig. 13.5).

BERBERIS × STENOPHYLLA
E F/I 1·8m (6ft) Trim after flowering. Suitable for most soils, including chalk; tolerant of pollution and salt. Produces pale orange flowers in spring.

BUXUS SEMPERVIRENS (box)
E F to 2·4m (8ft) Trim in August. There are many kinds of differing sizes and leaf patterns. The smallest is used for edging, dwarf box, *B. s. suffruticosa*, which rarely exceeds 60cm (2ft) whilst that most suited to hedges is *B. s. arborescens*. Suitable for a wide range of soils including chalk although it is best on a warm dry soil; tolerant of salt and pollution.

Fig. 13.5. *Berberis darwinii* is one of the best berberis for hedging purposes. It is covered in attractive golden yellow flowers in spring and bears an enormous crop of fruits in autumn

CARPINUS BETULUS (horn-beam) D F/I 6m (20ft) or more. Trim in August. It is suitable in most soils including chalk and will tolerate shade and pollution. Retains its brown leaves throughout the winter.

CHAMAECYPARIS LAWSONI-ANA (Lawson's cypress) E F 6m (20ft) or more. Trim in August. There are many cultivars which can be used for hedges, three of these are: 'Allumii', 'Erecta Viridis' and 'Green Hedger'. Tolerant of pollution, it will grow on most soils including chalk.

COTONEASTER FRANCHETII E F 2·7m (9ft) Trim in March. Suitable for a wide range of soils including chalk; tolerant of pollution. Produces pinkish flowers followed by red berries which are retained throughout winter.

COTONEASTER SIMONSII D F 2·4m (8ft) Trim in March. Suitable for a wide range of soils including chalk; white flowers followed by long-lasting, pinkish-red berries.

CRATAEGUS OXYACANTHA and **C. MONOGYNA (hawthorn)** D F 4·5m (15ft) or more. Trim in winter. For a gardener both species can be considered to be the same, making excellent hedges for all situations and can be kept to almost any size; thorns keep out undesirables. White or red flowers in May are followed by red berries.

× CUPRESSOCYPARIS LEY-LANDII E F/I to 6m (20ft) or more. Trim when required in August. A fast grower that will withstand full exposure to wind, so making a good windbreak; tolerant of salt and pollution. Plant small from the open ground.

CUPRESSUS MACROCARPA (monterey cypress) E F to 6m (20ft) or more. Trim in August. Tolerant of salt. Needs a good soil. Can be damaged by extreme cold weather or winds. Cannot withstand cutting back into old wood.

ELAEAGNUS × EBBINGII E F to 3m (10ft) Trim in August. Fast growing when young, it will tolerate salt and pollution. Suited to a wide range of soils and will grow in shade.

ELAEAGNUS PUNGENS E F 3m (10ft) Trim in August. There are a number of cultivars with golden variegated leaves. Suited to a wide range of soils. Tolerates shade, salt and pollution.

ESCALLONIA E F/I 2·4m (8ft) Trim in April. There are several species and many hybrids and cultivars all of which are suitable for hedges. Not suited to cold areas, they grow well near to the sea tolerating salt winds. All produce white or pink flowers in abundance.

EUONYMUS JAPONICUS (Japanese spindle bush) E F to 3m (10ft) Trim in August. There are many cultivars with different coloured leaves which have less vigour than the species. It is suited to a wide range of soils and is tolerant of salt.

FAGUS SYLVATICA (beech) D F 6m (20ft) and much more. Trim in August. Will grow on most soils including chalk as long as they are not too dry. Retains brown leaves over winter.

FUCHSIA MAGELLANICA D I to 1·8m (6ft) Trim in March. There are a number of forms of differing vigour. Well suited to growing near the sea where it needs a moist soil.

HIPPOPHAE RHAMNOIDES (sea buckthorn) D F/I 4·5m (15ft) Trim in March. It is to be found naturally on sand dunes exposed to the full force of sea gales. Female plants in the presence of males produce masses of orange fruits (Fig. 13.6).

HEBE BRACHYSIPHON (Veronica traversii) E F/I 1·8m (6ft) Trim in August. Tolerant of salt and pollution. Produces masses of white, tinged mauve flowers in June.

Fig. 13.6. *Hippophaë rhamnoides*, the sea-buckthorn, is sometimes grown as a hedge and is stunning in fruit. Both male and female bushes must be planted to obtain fruit

Fig. 13.7. *Hebe* makes a rather informal hedge

HEBE SALICIFOLIA E F/I 3m (10ft) Trim in April before new growth begins. The hardiest of species and tolerant of salt and pollution. It produces spikes of white tinged lilac flowers in summer (Fig. 13.7).

ILEX AQUIFOLIUM (holly) E F 3·6m (12ft) or more. Trim in August. There are many cultivars with varying leaf shape and colour patterns. It is suited to a wide range of soils, preferring one that remains moist. It will tolerate pollution and salt. The female will produce red berries when male plants are present.

LAURUS NOBILIS (bay) E F 3·6m (12ft) or more. Trim to shape in August with secateurs. The form 'Angustifolia' has smaller and narrower leaves and is the better type for hedges. Tolerant of salt and pollution but is unsuited to cold areas and exposure to cold winds; fragrant foliage.

LAVANDULA ANGUSTIFOLIA or **L. SPICA (common lavender)** E F 60cm (2ft) Trim after flowering or in April. Both names seem to be used for the same plants. There are many forms of differing vigour, compactness and flower colour. Will tolerate pollution and salt and whilst suited to most soils including chalk is best on one that is hot and dry. The stems of scented flowers produced above the fragrant foliage can reach 90cm (3ft) (Fig. 13.8).

LIGUSTRUM OVALIFOLIUM (privet) E F/I up to 3m (10ft) Although trimmed several times a year, cutting in August and perhaps a second time in March should be all that is necessary. The golden form is popular and there is one which has white variegation. Suitable for almost any kind of soil and tolerant of any adverse condition. As it is a fast grower and gross feeder, is undesirable for a small garden. Perhaps because it is the cheapest of hedging plants it has been vastly overplanted. As a pleasant change when space permits it can be grown informally and allowed to flower then being trimmed in winter.

LONICERA NITIDA E F 1·8m (6ft) Trim in August. Better on heavier soils.

Fig. 13.8. A lavender hedge.
Although often grown rather in
the manner of box edging,
lavender is really best trained as
a low mound when grown as a
hedge

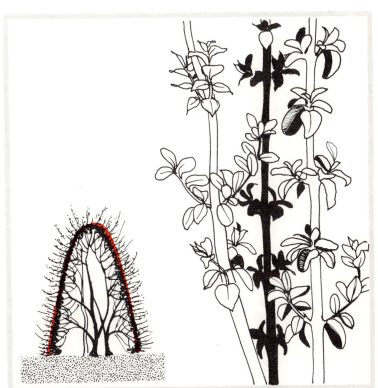

Fig. 13.9. A Lonicera hedge
showing the best shape for
pruning such a hedge

Can be damaged in a cold winter or with exposure to cold winds. Heavy snows can spoil its shape (Fig. 13.9).

MYRTUS COMMUNIS (myrtle)
E F/I 2·4m (8ft) Trim in late April as new growth is commencing. Will grow on a wide range of soils including chalk and is tolerant of salt. Unsuitable for cold areas or exposure to cold winds. White flowers are produced freely during the summer followed by blue-black fruits; foliage fragrant.

OLEARIA HAASTII
E F/I 1·8m (6ft) Trim in early April before new growth begins. Tolerant of salt and pollution. Produces masses of white daisy-flowers in summer.

OSMANTHUS (× osmarea) × BURKWOODII
E F/I 1·8m (6ft) Trim after flowering. Needs a moist soil; produces masses of sweetly scented white flowers in spring.

OSMANTHUS HETEROPHYLLUS
E F/I 3m (10ft) Trim in April with secateurs. Tolerant of salt and pollution and will grow in shade in a moist lime-free soil. In September produces sweetly scented white flowers.

PHILLYREA ANGUSTIFOLIA
E F 3m (10ft) Trim in August. Tolerant of a wide range of soils including chalk and will grow near the sea.

PITTOSPORUM TENUIFOLIUM
E F 3·6m (12ft) or more. Trim in August. Needs a moist soil, tolerant of salt but is unsuitable for cold areas.

POTENTILLA FRUTICOSA
D F/I 90cm (3ft) Trim in March. Suitable for a wide range of soils including chalk. Is used for edging and the many forms produce a succession of white, yellow or orange flowers throughout the summer.

PRUNUS CERASIFERA (cherry plum)
D F 4·5m (15ft) or more. Trim in winter. There is a purple-leafed form *P. c.* 'Atropurpurea' which is also good for hedges. Suitable for almost any soil, fast growing and withstands hard cutting. Produces white flowers before leaves followed by edible red fruits.

PRUNUS LAUROCERASUS (cherry laurel)
E F 4·5m (15ft) or more. Trim in August with secateurs. There are a number of forms of different vigour and leaf shape. Will grow on a wide range of soils and is tolerant of shade and pollution. It can be damaged in a very cold winter.

PRUNUS LUSITANICA (Portugal laurel)
E F 4·5m (15ft) or more. Trim in August with secateurs. Can be grown on a wide range of soils. Will tolerate shade or pollution.

PRUNUS SPINOSA (blackthorn or sloe)
E F up to 3·6m (12ft) Trim in winter. Tolerant of full exposure including sea gales and will grow on most soils including chalk. Spiney branches make an impenetrable hedge. White flowers in late winter are followed by blue-black fruits.

PYRACANTHA (firethorn)
E F 2·4m (8ft) Trim in April. All species suitable for making hedges to more or less the same height. Will grow on most soils and is tolerant of pollution. Its spines make an impenetrable hedge. Bunches of white flowers are followed by berries yellow, orange and red depending on species.

QUERCUS ILEX (holm oak)
E F 6·0 (20ft) or more. Trim with secateurs in August. Needs a good deep soil but will grow well where there is chalk; tolerant of sea winds. Needs to be planted small ex-pots.

RHODODENDRON PONTICUM
E F/I 3m (10ft) or more. Trim after flowering. Many of the stronger hybrid rhododendrons can be used equally well for informal hedges but cost is usually prohibitive. Needs a moist acid soil with plenty of organic matter. *Rh. ponticum* is tolerant of pollution.

ROSA (rose)
D I mostly 90cm (3ft) or less. Trim in winter or following flowering. Species:

Fig. 13.10. A rosemary hedge showing the more rounded shape to which it is best adapted when grown as a hedge

R. spinosissima, R. rubiginosa, R. rugosa. Shrub Roses: Penzance Briars, musks, burnets or rugosa. Floribundas: 'Frensham', 'Queen Elizabeth'. Hybrid Perpetuals: 'Hugh Dickson', 'Frau Karl Drushki', 'Zephryn Drouhin'.

ROSMARINUS OFFICINALIS (rosemary) E F/I to 1·8m (6ft) Trim after flowering (Fig. 13.10). There are a number of forms of differing vigour, habit and flower colour. Suitable for a wide range of soils including chalk but better on a hot dry one. A plant with fragrant foliage and coloured flowers that is suitable for seaside or towns. Can with hard cutting be used for edging.

SANTOLINA NEAPOLITANUM (lavender cotton) E F 60cm (2ft) Trim in August and after flowering for informal and formal and again in April for the latter.

TAMARIX (tamarisk) D F/I 3m (10ft) Trim in March except for *T. tetrandra* and

T. parviflora which are pruned after flowering. All species suitable for planting near to the sea but need regular hard pruning to keep tidy and well furnished at the base. There are spectacular flowers produced in abundance but their life is short.

TEUCRIUM CHAMAEDRYS (germander) E F 30cm (1ft) Trim in August or April. Suitable for a fragrant edging producing pink flowers during the summer.

THUJA PLICATA (western red cedar) E F 6·0m (20ft) or more. Trim in August. A fast growing tree needing a moist lime free soil; unsuitable for a small garden.

THYMUS VULGARIS (common thyme) E F 30cm (1ft) Trim in August or April. Suitable for a fragrant edging with pinkish flowers. Tolerant of pollution and salt. It is suited to most soils including chalk but is best on one which is warm and dry.

14 The Craft of Topiary

Topiary, an extreme form of pruning, is the trimming of bushes and trees to produce formal or bizarre shapes. It has a long history as a garden form and although more popular in continental Europe, especially Holland, it reached its zenith in this country during the 17th century. It was used then formally and blended well with statuary and garden ornaments of the period to form architectural designs. The only garden of this type extant from that period is that at Levens Hall in Westmorland which was planted in 1705. During the 18th century topiary went out of fashion when naturalism swept away formality but it returned to favour in the latter part of the Victorian era lingering into this century. Whilst it has had its fashions in garden design on the grand scale, it has retained its popularity with cottagers and latterly with owners of small gardens in towns and cities.

As a garden form it creates strong feelings varying from, at one extreme, those who consider it the ultimate in gardening skill to the other where people abhor it, yet can admire the perseverance of the gardener who created it. For those wishing to indulge in the art of topiary, it is a pastime where results are looked for in decades rather than years.

There are many kinds of shrubs and trees that can be treated as topiary subjects. *Myrtus communis* (myrtle), *Phillyrea angustifolia*, *Lonicera nitida*, *Cupressus macrocarpa* (monterey cypress), *C. sempervirens* (Italian cypress), *Ilex aquifolium* (holly), *Laurus nobilis* (bay) and *Thuja plicata* (western red cedar). The choice might be further extended as long as the foliage is small and evergreen so that in clipping, even faces result without ragged torn leaves. Today there are mostly two kinds of plants in use: box and yew. Box is slower growing and the smaller

of the two but to some has a less sombre appearance. The ultimate shape will depend on personal choice but those of geometric form have always been popular; cubes, pyramids, domes, spheres, cones, pillars both round and square in cross-section and archways which are modifications of pillars. The other type which has great appeal is some kind of animal or bird; the peacock is often attempted.

It is preferable to start from scratch by planting a young shrub. A two-year-old bush, whilst smaller, is cheaper, and will establish more quickly and very soon overtake an older more expensive plant. The ground where it is to be planted should be thoroughly prepared. A square $1 \cdot 8 \times 1 \cdot 8$m ($6 \times 6$ft) should be double dug with as much organic matter as possible incorporated in the lower spit. Tread the ground and remove surplus soil so that the plant finishes up in a slight depression which will make subsequent watering easy.

Before planting in late March or April apply to the prepared area a dressing of a general fertilizer of 227g (8oz) and rake in. Following planting, encourage rapid growth by removing competition, either weeds or pests and water during dry periods. Every year repeat the application of fertilizer at the same rate ensuring it is spread out evenly over the soil that is occupied by the roots. In early years until established a mulch spread around the plant will be beneficial.

The first trimming will take place in the following August and will continue in the same month annually. Leave the growing points untouched but trim back all side shoots. In the first year clip back quite hard to encourage the development of a well-furnished base as for a hedge. In subsequent years trim more lightly aiming to produce the shape required. Cubes, pillars and archways will have vertical sides but in all other forms sides will be tapering. Fancy figures such as animals and birds are not trained until a suitable base has been produced.

Training

Spiral

Plant a young bush against a stout stake about 8cm (3in) in diameter. Retain only a single leader and in the following August wind the new growth around the stake, tie in position and pinch back side shoots. Allow the single leader to continue growing in the next season and in August again, wind the new growth around the stake. Thin side shoots so that what remain do not overcrowd each other. These are trained in such a way that there is a tapering in length from base to apex to produce a narrow elongated cone. If an open spiral is required, use three stakes placed close together and wind the new growth around these as though there was only one, training as already mentioned.

Interrupted cone

To produce a cake-stand effect following the furnishing of a well-clothed base, a single leader must be selected and retained. The different levels can be produced by allowing the bush to grow to a considerable size and then removing a number of side shoots from the trunk around the circumference at different levels (Fig. 14.1). This method is not ideal as each tier can be poorly furnished with leaves. It is better to train in each tier as the bush is growing. When the leader reaches 1·35m (4½ft) retain the leader with the side branches immediately below and then completely remove for a distance of about 30cm (1ft) all other side branches. The leader is allowed to grow on until with all side branches retained for another 1·35m (4½ft) and the same treatment is repeated. This process continues until there are enough tiers.

Meanwhile the branches between the tiers are trimmed in such a way as to produce the outline of a cone.

Fig. 14.1. Topiary shapes: a traditional interrupted cone

Fig. 14.2. An archway. Strictly, this is topiary work, although a lot of people would undertake it without realizing that it is so

Fig. 14.3. Fixing wires into position and tying in a number of shoots

Fig. 14.4. Shoots tied into position, showing the peacock taking shape

Fig. 14.5. Completed bird

Archway

Two plants are needed, one on either side of a pathway. Do allow for eventual increase in width, by planting sufficiently far apart so that there will be no obstruction to pedestrians at some future date. Insert a stout stake to the inner height of the arch for each plant before planting and across the top fix wooden battens or thick gauge wire. During the training trim the bushes to produce vertical sides retaining and encouraging several leaders. When these exceed the height of the stakes, in August pull down the leading shoots until they meet and secure to the cross pieces. If they are not long enough, pull in and tie loosely so that they face each other and in the following year there will be sufficient growth to meet when the shoots can be pulled right down and tied into position. For a narrow archway stakes are not necessary for when the leaders are tall enough they can be brought together and tied to each other. Just as the under part of the archway can be flat or in an arc so the upper and outer part can be trained in the same way (Fig. 14.2).

Peacock

Train in the early years so as to produce a cone. When the basal part of the cone has been formed, take the leaders and separate into two unequal bunches to produce the tail and the other, the head and body. Push through the basal part of the cone and into the ground, a long stake 2·5–5cm (1–2in) in diameter. Fix firmly to its end a circle of thick gauge wire 60–90cm (2–3ft) in diameter (*see* Fig. 14.3). Spread out the shoots of the larger bunch and having evenly spaced them out, tie to the wire. It will make tying easier if some parallel wires are fixed across the base of the circle. Meanwhile a second small circle of wire is fixed in the opposite direction from the first and the other bunch of leaders is tied loosely around it. Continue to encourage development of shoots that are fixed to these wires training the tail as a large fan whilst the other bunch is formed into the body and head (Fig. 14.4). Inspect all ties annually retying whenever necessary to ensure that shoots are not strangled. Once the framework has formed and branches will have been trained into fixed positions the stake with its wires can be removed (Fig. 14.5).

Subsequent training

Once the framework of any figure has been established, its outline must be kept sharp by regular trimming. For simple geometric figures, cubes, pillars, pyramids, cones and pillars, power cutters can be used, for curved surfaces and intricate figures use sharp shears. By the time the training is complete, the gardener should be sufficiently skilled and have developed a good eye, capable of producing sophisticated shapes.

15 Old Trees

Caution and conservation

It is not uncommon for a garden to contain old trees in need of some care and attention. Neglected fruit trees are all too common and the means of restoring them to better bearing are dealt with in the chapters devoted to the fruit. If such trees are in a semi-derelict state the most sensible course of action may be to fell them and replant with new bush trees that will be more fruitful and easier to manage. It is important, however, not to replant on exactly the same site.

In this chapter we are concerned more with the ornamental tree that is a garden feature and which could not be replaced to the same effect within the lifetime of the gardener. It should be noted also that a garden owner may not fell a large forest-type tree without the permission of the local authority, and that permission may only be granted if the tree is proved to be seriously diseased or to be a danger to property. A tree that obscures light may be cut back by the owner, or he may even be required to cut it back because someone else's light is obstructed. Restrictions on the removal of trees are wise in terms of preserving our landscape. Trees are part of our heritage, and it can be argued that we are merely custodians with a duty to preserve and enhance the landscape for future generations.

If pruning is understood broadly to mean 'cutting back' and remedying faults in tree structure, there are several reasons why the gardener may need to apply these treatments. In doing so he enters the realm of arboriculture which is a highly professional field. This point is made because there are limits to what the amateur should do, and beyond them the expert should be called upon. Clearly the removal of large sections of a tall tree can be dangerous. Full-time tree-surgeons are equipped with suitable gear and follow a safety code in their work.

But the amateur should be able to restrict growth by root pruning, to cleanly remove obstructive low branches and then protect the wound, and to fill a cavity in the fork of a tree. Bracing a weak cleft with a bolted bar or cable may also be within his capability.

Root pruning

Root pruning, whilst formerly practised, is rarely undertaken today: it is a technique used to restrict the vigour of fruit trees and so encourage bearing, but it can also be applied to limit the growth of ornamental trees. It is best carried out over two winters, tackling one semi-circle of root area one year, the other the next (Fig. 15.1). The point at which to expose the roots is below the furthest spread of the branches. At this point start to dig a semi-circular trench until thick roots are uncovered. These are the tap roots that need to be severed: do not remove fine feeding roots. As a rule of thumb, sever only those roots that are thicker than a broom handle—though tap roots of fruit trees may be thinner than this. Conifers produce masses of fibrous roots and some of these may be chopped out to control vigour.

Tree surgery

Branch removal must be thorough. If dead wood is being removed the cut must be made back into healthy tissue. Always cut a lateral branch flush with the main branch; this will usually mean first cutting away most of the branch and then removing the stub. Do not allow a cut surface to face upwards and so collect water, but slant it so that rain will be

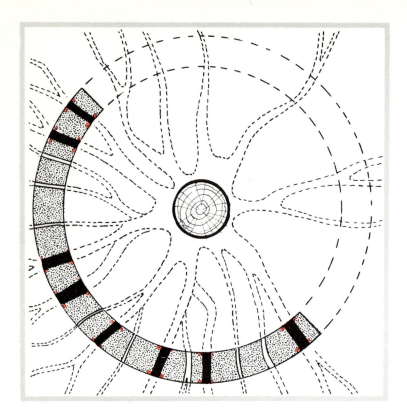

Fig. 15.1. Root pruning showing above a plan view from above and below a sectional view through the trench from the side

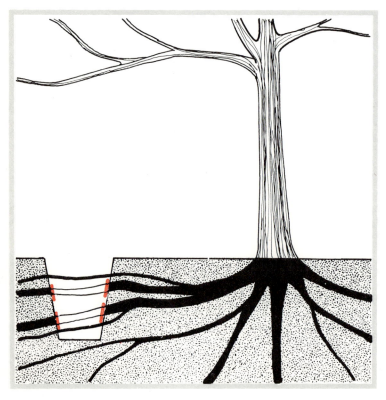

140

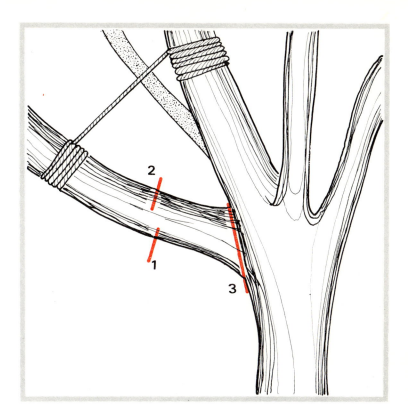

Fig. 15.2. The removal of a heavy branch from old tree. A sequence of cuts is numbered and the limb to be removed is securely tied to a stronger branch before the cut is made

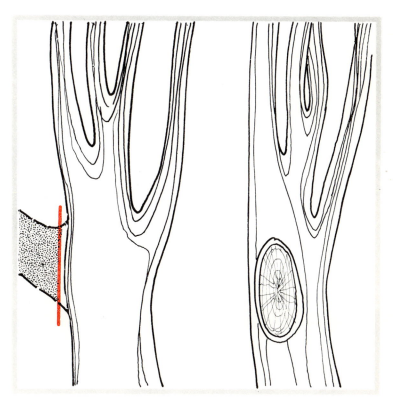

Fig. 15.3. Removal of a large branch showing how any stubby material should be pared away so that the cut is flush with the main stem

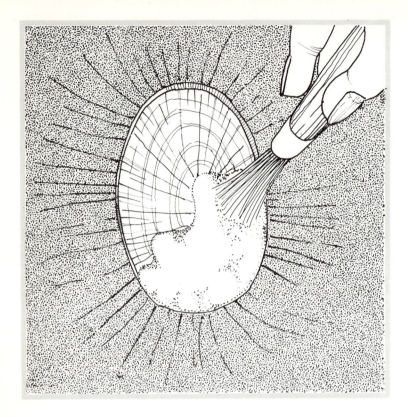

Fig. 15.4. Applying a pruning compound to a large cut. The pruning compound acts as an artificial bark until the tree forms a callus over the wound

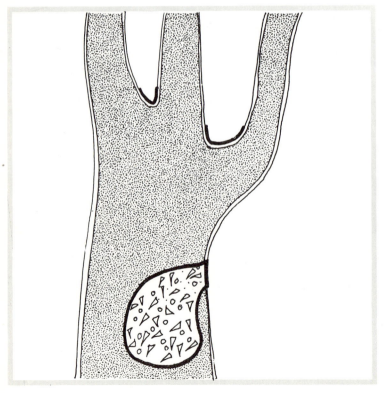

Fig. 15.5. Cavity and cleft treatment in old trees. The cavity should be filled with a coarse concrete mixture and made flush with the bark of the tree

thrown off. If several amputations are necessary, spread the job over more than one year in order to ease the shock to the tree, and to limit the production of weak 'water shoots' that follows any hard pruning.

The safest time for most tree surgery is during the dormant season from October to March. Trees cut in active growth will 'bleed' sap, especially beech, sycamore, maple and birch, and this prevents wound healing and invites the entry of disease. There are two exceptions to this rule on dormant pruning: *Prunus* species (cherries, for example) are pruned in May or June because of a specific disease risk, and walnut is cut in leaf because it bleeds less then.

To avoid tearing bark from the main trunk during branch removal, a heavy branch should first be undercut. Make the cut at least 30cm (12in) from the final flush-cut to the extent of half the thickness of the limb. Then cut from the top slightly in front of the undercut (Fig. 15.2). Support the branch with a rope slung over a higher stout limb before severing, so that it can be lowered to the ground. Remove the stub flush with the main trunk or primary branch (Fig. 15.3).

Obviously a saw needs to be stout and sharp for this work, and a bow saw is generally the most manageable type. The flush-cut should be trimmed smooth with a sharp knife, any dead wood being cut out. A cleanly pared surface, especially at the edges, will permit the growth zone (cambium) just inside the bark to generate wound-healing tissue that will ultimately close the wound. To ensure healthy wound healing, however, all cuts should be covered with a wound dressing compound (Fig. 15.4). Apply the compound as directed when the surface is dry. New tissue will form behind this antiseptic cover.

The same material is applied to a hollow or exposed cleft in a tree once the surfaces have been pared clean and dried. To fill in a large hollow in a trunk after wound dressing has been applied to the surfaces, use a stiff cement mix (Fig. 15.5). Allow space for the 'repair' tissue to grow and cover the cavity opening.

A split fork, fairly common in beech, may be bolted and braced. This entails drilling through both limbs, passing the bolts through plates on the outer surfaces and fixing a rod or cable between.

16 Pruning of Greenhouse Plants

In this book only the commonest genera of greenhouse plants have been included from which the pruning of no more than one or two species have been discussed. Plants which have been omitted are those that are: propagated annually from seed or cuttings, require no pruning, and plants which though also grown under glass are to be found outside in the garden and from which the pruning in no way differs from that already discussed earlier in this book.

Abbreviations in use

- T   Trees
- S   Shrubs
- C   Climbers

1   Frost-free greenhouses
2   Temperate—winter minimum 7°C (45°F)
3   Tropical—winter minimum 16°C (60°F)

Depending on size of greenhouse and plant vigour, subjects may be grown in pots or borders. As with shrubs outside, following hard pruning, feed border plants well whilst those in pots should be top-dressed and fed or repotted.

A number of plants usually grown as bushes can be trained as standards, the method being described under *Fuchsia*.

ABUTILON 1 S *A. megapotamicum*, though best in a border trained up a wall or trellis, is suitable for growing as a pot plant which will flower throughout most of the year; there is a form with mottled golden variegated leaves. Usually dried off in winter, all shoots are cut hard back before new growth commences in the spring. *A.* 'Savitzii' has leaves with a broad band of intense white variegation. It is slow growing and usually kept to a single stem; pruning consists of cutting back hard bare or gaunt stems and retraining in a single shoot. *A. striatum* 'Thomsonii' is a strong grower with mottled golden variegated leaves although the dull orange bell-shaped flowers have some attraction. Prune back all shoots in early spring just before growth recommences. There are numerous abutilons of hybrid origin which have large showy flowers in a number of colours. These produce their flowers on current season's growth and all are trimmed back hard before growth commences in the spring. It is common to train the stronger growing kinds as standards either for use in summer bedding or to give height to a display in a greenhouse.

ACACIA 1 S/T There are many species, some being shrubs others trees. The smaller kinds of shrubs can be grown in pots but the more vigorous and the trees need to be planted in a border. Pot subjects are pruned after

Fig. 16.1. *Allamanda*

flowering when those shoots which have flowered are cut hard back and any others thinned. *A. dealbata* the florists' mimosa is a vigorous grower and only suited to the largest greenhouse. It needs annual pruning to keep within bounds and to prevent it from reaching the roof where its blooms are mostly out of sight and squashed against the glass. Following blooming, remove those branches which have flowered and reduce the height of all stems so that they are well clear of the glass and remain so throughout the growing season. During training ensure that the lower part of the tree is kept well clothed with shoots.

ACALYPHA 3 s *A. hispida* is grown for its long red tassel-like flowers but *A. wilkesiana* in one of its many forms, for coloured leaves. Well suited to pot culture, grown either as a bush or to a single stem, they are usually propagated from cuttings every second or third year. Pruning takes place in March when stems are thinned and those remaining cut hard back.

ALLAMANDA 3 c Can be grown as a pot plant but gives a better display in a border.

Water is withheld during winter and before restarting into growth again in March, shoots are cut back by half and some thinning is carried out. Pot subjects need more drastic thinning retaining three shoots and reducing by a third (Fig. 16.1).

ARISTOLOCHIA 2/3 c There are many different species of which perhaps *A. elegans* (Dutchman's pipe) is best known. Most are fast growers needing plenty of space and so are better suited for border cultivation against a wall or trellis. Pruning consists of thinning shoots drastically after flowering and retraining only enough to cover their support.

BOUGAINVILLEA 2/3 c Although there are many cultivars these belong to two species, *B. glabra* (Fig. 16.2) and *B. spectabilis*, the former tolerates cooler conditions, is less vigorous and can be grown in pots. During winter, water is withheld which results in leaf drop. Before restarting into growth in March or April, prune back all side shoots to two or three buds of the main stem. Retain only about four of these, removing always the oldest, and

145

Fig. 16.2. *Bougainvillea*

reduce in length by a third or half. *B. glabra*, of which there are many forms, does well in a border with the support of a trellis or wall. Pruning consists of thinning out growth and cutting back all side shoots to two or three buds and reducing the main stems. *B. spectabilis* is too vigorous for pot culture and needs to be grown in a border; prune as for the other species.

BORONIA 1 s There are a few species grown in a cool greenhouse but the favourite, because of its fragrance, is the reddish brown *B. megastigma*. Small enough for pot culture it is pruned after flowering when all shoots which have bloomed are cut back and any remaining thinned.

BELOPERONE *see* **DREGERELLA**

BUDDLEIA 1 s A few species too tender for outdoor culture are grown under glass for winter flowering. *B. asiatica* has very fragrant spikes of white flowers whilst those of *B.* 'Margaret Pike' are yellow. After blooming those shoots which have flowered are cut hard back and the others reduced. *B.* (*Nicodemia*) *mada-*

gascariensis is a border plant being trained up a wall or trellis. Pruning takes place after flowering when all shoots are cut back to within two or three buds of a framework.

CAMELLIA 1 s Although *C. japonica* and its very many cultivars are hardy out of doors in most of Britain, they are often grown in pots, tubs or in borders to protect and keep their flowers clean in inclement winter and early spring weather; during summer, pots and tubs are often stood outside. Pruning follows flowering when there is dead-heading, thinning of crowded growth and trimming to shape. *C. reticulata* and its forms is grown outside only in the mildest parts of the country and is really considered a greenhouse plant for flower buds are easily damaged, like foliage, by cold weather. More untidy in growth than *C. japonica*, some trimming to shape is usually required following flowering.

CODIAEUM (croton) 2/3 s Grown in pots for their attractively patterned leaves. Little pruning except to cut back hard, overlong shoots, any which have lost their lower

146

Fig. 16.3. The shrimp plant
Dregerella (*Beloperone*)
guttata

leaves and to trim to shape; carry out in late winter.

CYTISUS 1 s *C.* × *spachianus* (*C. racemosus*, *Genista fragrans*) is grown as a pot plant for its deliciously scented yellow flowers. After blooming cut back those shoots which have flowered.

DREGERELLA (Beloperone) 2 s *D. guttata* (shrimp plant) is grown as a pot plant for its long display of coloured bracts. Cut back hard and trim to shape just before new growth commences in early spring (Fig. 16.3).

ERICA (heath) 1 s Once the South African heaths were popular Christmas house plants but today they seem to be out of fashion and yet they are useful plants for winter display in a cool greenhouse. Following flowering, lightly trim all shoots which have bloomed; avoid cutting into old wood.

EUPHORBIA 2 s A very large family to which many greenhouse succulents belong;

these can be cut back to ground-level if they become top heavy in pots or when they reach the greenhouse roof if planted in a border. *E. pulcherrima* (poinsettia) is used for winter display and is a popular Christmas house plant. As the colour of the bracts begins to dull, water is withheld and the plants are dried off. In May or June, the plants are cut back hard and restarted into growth.

FICUS 1/2 s/т A number of shrubs are grown in pots or borders as foliage plants. They need no pruning except to trim to shape when at their most dormant for if pruned when in growth there is a tendency to bleed. *F. elastica* (India rubber plant) a popular house plant is usually kept to a single stem. If this reaches the ceiling of a room or greenhouse roof, loses many of its lower leaves or becomes top heavy it is cut back hard and resulting growth is usually trained to a single stem; cut back when not in active growth. *F. pumila* (creeping fig) has a number of forms well suited to growing in a cool shaded place such as a north wall or under staging; can be grown as a pot plant. Very little pruning is necessary except to keep within bounds and to remove stems which have become bare of leaves.

FUCHSIA 1 s The showy hybrids of which there are many hundreds are greenhouse plants for cultivation in pots, baskets and borders whether as free-standing shrubs or trained against a wall, up a trellis or wires. During winter plants are kept dry when most leaves fall. Before being restarted into growth in March or April; basket plants if being retained for a second year are cut hard back; those in pots are treated similarly with a thinning of weak and crowded shoots and wall-trained plants have all side shoots shortened back to two buds of a framework.

Training of standards

Select and pot a rooted cutting of a strong growing cultivar. Secure the stem to a stake, tying at frequent intervals and pinching out side shoots. Keep growing and pot on as each container fills with roots. When the stem reaches 90cm (3ft) pinch out the growing point and allow a number of pairs of side branches to develop. At the end of that growing season the standard is dried off and pruned just before being restarted into growth; shorten back to a third all side shoots removing any that are weak.

GARDENIA 3 s Usually grown in pots for the powerful scent of white wax flowers. Little pruning except to dead-head and trim to shape after flowering (Fig. 16.4).

GREVILLEA 1 s/t There are many species which produce shrubs of varying sizes and trees. The smaller kinds are well suited to growing in pots and pruning of these consists of trimming to shape after flowering, thinning and reducing any long shoots when out of flower and not in active growth. *G. robusta* (silky oak) although making a tree is grown as a pot plant (Fig. 16.5) to a single stem for its attractive foliage being used for greenhouse display or in summer bedding as a dot plant.

Fig. 16.4. *Gardenia*

Fig. 16.5. *Grevillea robusta*

Fig. 16.6. *Hibiscus rosa-sinensis*

149

When plants become bare at the base or over tall, cut hard back and retrain a single shoot.

HIBISCUS 3 s The most commonly grown species under glass is one of the many forms of *H. rosa-sinensis* (Fig. 16.6) with its large showy fleeting flowers of many colours. Mostly grown as pot plants although when space permits better flowering will occur from cultivation in a border. Pot plants are cut hard back just before new growth begins in late winter whilst border plants are thinned of crowded and weak shoots and those remaining are shortened by a third or a half.

HOYA 3 c *H. carnosa* is grown in the smallest pot possible to restrict its growth and induce freer flowering (Fig. 16.7). Care should be taken not to cut off old flowers for new ones emerge from the same place on the stems. Little pruning except to cut out surplus shoots when not in growth and to train in twining stems by looping and tying them to the top of their support. *H. bella* is a small growing plant with lax stems and whilst grown as a pot plant makes a good subject for a hanging basket. After flowering thin out surplus shoots and trim to shape.

JACARANDA 2 s/t Although one of the most beautiful of flowering trees is too big for all but the largest conservatories. Mostly it is grown to a single stem in a pot for its delicate fern-like foliage. When the base of the stem becomes bare or the plant becomes ungainly, it is cut hard back just before restarting into growth and although all the resulting growths may be retained, most often they are reduced to one.

JASMINUM 1/2/3 s/c There are a number of species that are glasshouse plants all of which are vigorous and need border cultivation. Perhaps *J. polyanthum* which produces its whitish sweetly scented flowers in winter is the best known. This should be pruned following flowering when the shoots which have born blooms are removed, the tangle of growth

Fig. 16.7. *Hoya carnosa*

thinned leaving only enough shoots to fill the allotted space and all of these are reduced by a third. Of the other species, those which flower in winter are pruned after flowering whilst the summer flowerers just before new growth commences in spring.

LANTANA 1 s The most commonly grown is *L. camara*. Grown as a pot plant it has a long flowering season and as autumn advances, water is withheld and bare stemmed plants are kept dry throughout the winter. Before restarting into growth in early spring, all stems are cut back hard and weak shoots removed. The strongest kinds can be trained as standards.

LEPTOSPERMUM 1 s The coloured and double flowered forms of *L. scoparium* need greenhouse protection to give their best flowering display. The dwarf kinds are suited to pot culture but others dislike pots and are better growing in a border either free standing or trained against a wall or trellis. After flower-ing remove shoots which have bloomed, thin drastically and trim to shape.

NERIUM (oleander) 1 s A free-flowering shrub for pot or border culture. Just prior to commencement of growth, thin out weak and crowded shoots and trim to shape, shortening any overlong stems (Fig. 16.8).

NICODEMIA *see* **BUDDLEIA**

PASSIFLORA (passion flower) 2 c Mostly vigorous climbers better as border plants trained up a wall, trellis or wires. At the end of winter as new growth is about to start, thin out crowded shoots, reducing until there is sufficient to fill the allotted space and those retained should have a third of their stems removed.

PELARGONIUM 1/2 s Mistakenly referred to as geraniums which is the generic name for a group of hardy herbaceous plants. The commonest kind called zonals are much

Fig. 16.8. *Nerium oleander* needs to be pruned hard to flower well. All parts of the flower are poisonous, and care should be taken not to get the white milky sap in cuts or near the eyes

151

used in bedding and can be grown for flowers, foliage or both. These kinds and other cultivars are also used for greenhouse display and make suitable house plants although too often these are seen as straggly plants, badly needing pruning.

During the winter house plants are dried off as are those in the colder greenhouses. Before they are restarted into growth the plants need to be cut hard back. The same treatment is given to those plants growing in warmer houses which are not dried off, the timing of this depends on when the main flowering is required. Regal pelargoniums unlike the zonal types have only one flowering and these are cut back hard after the blooms have finished. Scented leaved pelargoniums (also called geraniums) cover a number of species and these are cut hard back as new growth is about to restart in early spring.

PLUMBAGO 12 s *P. capensis* makes a beautiful pot plant with a long succession of pale blue flowers. In winter plants may be dried off and before growth recommences, trim to shape, cut out weak growth and shorten back all shoots. As this flowers almost non-stop through summer and autumn some dead-heading should be carried out to keep plants tidy. Can be trained as a standard.

POINSETTIA 2s Frequently seen at Christmas, and grown for their large scarlet bracts. When these have fallen, cut back stems to within 15cm (6in) of the pot. Dust the cut ends with powdered charcoal to halt bleeding. About April or May shoots 8–10cm (3–4in) long can be taken as cuttings to raise fresh plants (Fig. 16.9). (See also *Euphorbia*.)

SOLANUM 1/2 s/c Most of the species grown under glass are climbers which have too much vigour for pot culture and are better in a border trained up a wall or trellis. Whilst still dormant in winter thin out excessive growth so that what remains is uncrowded and will comfortably cover the allotted space. Shorten back all shoots remaining to a half or even a third.

Fig. 16.9. Poinsettia: *Euphorbia pulcherrima*. If these are cut hard back once the bracts have lost their colour and kept fairly dry for a while it is possible to get them to produce another set of bracts the following season. In the wild they will make shrubs as much as 2·4m (8ft) tall so there is no reason why they should not do the same if treated carefully. Homes are not moist or warm enough for those bought as house plants to produce flowers satisfactorily for a second time

Fig. 16.10. *Streptosolen jamesonii*

Fig. 16.11. *Tibouchina semidecandra*

STEPHANOTIS 3 c Although grown as a pot plant there is a greater abundance of flowers from those grown in a border. Pot plants are pruned when dormant with a drastic thinning of shoots and the long growths are looped and tied back to the tops of their support. Border plants are thinned and trimmed to shape with overlong shoots cut back when not in active growth.

STREPTOSOLEN 1 s A shrub of ungainly habit which needs frequent pinching when growing to keep tidy and in shape (Fig. 16.10). It gives its best display planted in a border but is good as a pot plant and may be used as a dot plant in bedding. At the end of the season, water is withheld and most of the leaves fall. Before starting into growth reduce shoots by half, thin out weak shoots and trim to shape. Can be trained to a standard.

TIBOUCHINA 1 s Of lax habit this shrub is better in a border trained against a wall or trellis although it can be grown as a pot plant. Prune following its flowering when those shoots which have bloomed are shortened back, the same treatment afforded to long non-flowering shoots and trim to shape (Fig. 16.11).

LEGAL ASPECTS OF PRUNING

17 The Law on Pruning

The legal principles behind the law on pruning are somewhat obscure, but thankfully the rules of law themselves are less difficult and the way in which the prudent occupier of land should behave in this respect is clear enough.

The first—and paramount—commandment of the law, and also of good neighbourliness, is not to let the branches or shoots from any kind of plant project over the boundary between your property and someone else's. The growth of such a projection may involve what the law calls a trespass, an interference with someone else's possession of land (a possession which extends to the column of space above the surface, in theory to an infinite height. Or it may involve what the law calls a nuisance, the wrongful allowing of the escape of something harmful into someone else's land. But the precise classification is only of interest to academic lawyers. What is important to you is that your neighbour has a right to take action, by himself or through the courts, in respect of such projecting branches.

What are the remedies available to him? He can, without any notice, simply lop off the offending branches, just as he can sever roots from any of your trees that have spread on to his land. This is called the remedy of abatement. It must be exercised with some care, and a nice judgment as to where exactly the boundary between his land and yours is. If he is over-zealous and wreaks damage on the branches which properly and lawfully remain on your side of the fence, or whatever it is that demarcates his garden from yours, then he must compensate you for the value of the damage that he has done, if any, and, if necessary, you could take him to court and get a judgment for the appropriate sum. But the other matter that the abator must bear in mind is that if he resorts to self-help in this way, he cannot pursue an action in the courts even for past damage caused by the nuisance from the branches—not, as we shall see, that there are many occasions where a sensible man would resort to law.

One interesting point—what he cuts off remains yours, not his. If, for example, he cuts off an overhanging branch, heavy with ripe, golden plums, and then eats them all for supper, he must in law pay you their value. However, and this may strike you as odd, you have, it appears, no right to go on to his property and take the plums, or whatever, back; and he commits no wrong in refusing you permission to do so. There are old and obscure dicta of learned judges that give some basis for the opposite view, and certainly you can enter someone else's land to retake your belongings if they came on to his land by accident, eg falling fruit; but the weight of authority favours the proposition that his rights to control who may or may not come on to his property are more important than your rights to your possessions. It may be, however, that the obscurity of the law reflects the fact that in a common-sense world it has never been necessary to decide that particular point. Your neighbour would probably allow you on to his land for this limited purpose as you would him on to yours; in the same way, he would probably ask you to cut back your branches before he took the law (with the law's approval) into his own hands. In the majority of these common-or-garden cases the law may define what is right and what is wrong, but no one seriously imagines that its cumbersome and expensive machinery will be set into operation to remedy some trivial complaint. Indeed there may be a right of abatement where no action for damages will lie (although of course the reverse cannot be true). That is because damage is of the essence of the action for nuisance, and unless a plaintiff can prove some genuine harm, interference with his use or enjoyment of his own property, or some more serious form of physical damage to his possessions or person, then he will get no damages from a court of law. He may succeed in establishing a technical infringement of his air space, but he will probably have to pay his own costs, and even yours as well.

There are instances, however, where significant loss or damage can be caused by an overhanging branch or bough, nor least where your property adjoins a highway. The rule has been stated in this way in the leading textbook: 'If damage is done owing to the collapse of the projection on the highway or by some other mischief traceable to it, the occupier of the premises on which it stood is liable if he knew of the defect or, on investigation, ought to have known of it.' The same rule holds good if one substitutes the phrase 'on his neighbour's land' for the phrase 'on the highway'.

The duty to avoid causing damage by overhanging branches is not then an absolute one; the occupier is not an insurer. His obligation is only to take reasonable care. In one case the occupier of land was held not liable when the branch of a beech tree growing on his land and overhanging a highway suddenly broke off owing to a hidden defect not discoverable by any reasonable inspection and damaged the plaintiff's motor coach which was passing along the highway—a case which one commentator said in a learned journey 'saved the beautiful hedgerows of the English countryside'. But in another case the National Trust was held liable in negligence in failing to fell a dangerous tree near a highway, as this body had means of knowing it was diseased. So if you have any big trees that could, if they toppled over, strike a passing pedestrian, cyclist or motorist (or for that matter your neighbour's children playing football in his garden), make as sure as you can that it isn't going rotten inside; or if you have a straggling bough that just could be a traffic hazard, play safe and cut it off. But don't worry just because a few branches project innocently a little way over the highway. There is no one like your postulated officious neighbour who can come along and cut it down.

Finally if you do have problems of this sort with your neighbour, first try talking it out; then, possibly, consult a Citizens Advice Bureau, write to an advice column of a newspaper, or consult a solicitor. But don't go to court unless you have to. It is an expensive business unless you qualify for legal aid. And most judges quite rightly take the view that disputes between neighbours are best kept out of the courts altogether. But if by some mischance someone claims that your overhanging bough has caused a serious accident, then go to a solicitor at once. He will know how to handle these matters better than you.

Summary

You can cut down any branches that overhang your own property, but only up to your own boundary

What you cut off belongs to the person from whose tree or bush the branch grew. If it is of any value, eg if it bears ripe fruit, you ought to give it back to him

You are liable for any damage to person or property, or for any inconvenience, caused by your overhanging branches if you ought to have realised that they could create a danger or cause trouble. So do take care, especially where you have trees that abut a highway

If any serious problems arise, go to a solicitor. But try and solve minor disputes by a sensible chat with your neighbour

157

Glossary

Apical bud Terminal bud of a shoot, usually of the leading or main shoot

Balled roots A method by which evergreen trees and shrubs, conifers and some deciduous trees and shrubs are offered for sale. A portion of soil with the plant's root system is wrapped in hessian or polythene

Basal shoot Those rising from near ground-level

Biennial bearing A term used to denote fruit trees that bear heavily one year but scarcely at all in the next

Big bud A pest which attacks black and red currants causing the winter buds to become abnormally enlarged

Bleeding The oozing of sap from a cut resulting from pruning

Bracts Leaf-like structures on a flower stem which may be coloured and so resemble petals

Callus tissue Corky cells produced by a plant to seal a wound

Cambium A layer of cells situated beneath the bark capable of being stimulated into division following wounding to form callus prior to rooting

Canes (a) Stems of biennial duration produced by many species of Rubus
(b) Dried stems of bamboos used in a garden as plant supports

Conifer A group of woody plants, usually evergreens, that are in the main cone bearing

Coral spot A disease which attacks both dead and living wood having orange or coral coloured fructifications

Cordon A single trunk which bears fruit spurs

Crown (of a tree) The framework of the branch system of a mature tree

159

Cultivar   Cultivated variety; one that has arisen under cultivation—often abbreviated to cv

Cutting back   The removal of a considerable portion of the branches of a tree or shrub

Dead-heading   Removal of dead or fading flowers and the developing fruits

Deciduous   A term which describes those trees and shrubs which shed their leaves in the autumn

Dehorning   The removal of some old sound branches from within the framework of a tree

Die back   Death of a branch or part of a branch

Dormancy period   A state of rest within a plant

Double cordon   A cordon having two stems arising from a single trunk

Espalier   A method of training, usually a fruit tree against a wall or support in which one or more pairs of opposite branches are trained horizontally; each tier of branches having fruit spurs

Evergreen   A plant which retains its leaves for a period of longer than twelve months

Extension growth   Growth produced from a terminal bud

Fan   A method of training a shrub or tree, either fruiting or ornamental, against a wall or support where all the branches radiate from a short central trunk

Fastigiate   All branches growing vertically, parallel to the main trunk

Feathering   Cutting back of side shoots along young main stems to two or three buds

Feathers   Short twigs coming naturally from a young main stem

Feeding roots   Very fine roots on the outer perimeter of a root system that are capable of absorbing water and mineral nutrients in solution

Fireblight   A disease which attacks many woody members of the rose family (Rosaceae). In June or July dead shoots with dead blackened leaves attached can be seen, giving the appearance that branches have been burnt

Framework   The formation of branches in the crown of a tree

Framework building   The training and building up of the crown of a tree

Fruit bud   A bud which will produce a flower as distinct from a growth bud which produces another shoot

Graft   The joining together of two different plants to form a single new individual, having the root system of one plant and the aerial part of another

Growing point   A terminal bud

Growth bud   A bud which will produce a shoot as distinct from a fruit bud which will produce a flower

Half-standard   A tree having a clear stem of 1·35m (4½ft) on top of which the branching system develops; 90cm (3ft) in roses

Hard pruning   The removal of a large amount of wood from a tree or shrub

Lateral   A side shoot

Leader   A leading portion of a main branch

Leg   A short clear length of main stem on a shrub before branching is allowed to take place

Maiden   A single stem of one season's growth resulting from a graft

Oblique cordon   A cordon trained at an angle below the vertical usually between 60° and 45°

Pinching out   Removal of young shoots with the fingers

Pleaching   Training the framework of a tree to produce a screen or archway

Pollarding   Cutting back the main branches of a tree close to where they arise from the trunk

Pyramid   The method of training a fruit tree in which each tier of branches is composed of shorter branches than the tier below

Renewal pruning   A type of pruning practised on apples and pears in which there is a succession of shoots, fruit buds and branches and where the fruit is borne on laterals rather than spurs

Replacement leader   The selection and training of a young shoot to form part of the framework so that an older leader can be removed

Reversion   (a) A term used to denote a condition on a variegated plant where green shoots grow away at the expense of the variegated (b) A term used to describe any tree that is changing back to the original species of variety from which the sport first arose

Reversion (disease)	A virus disease of red and blackcurrants
Ripe wood	A branch or shoot that is thoroughly lignified
Rod	A main stem of a grapevine and some allied ornamental species and genera
Root bound	A condition which results from a plant being too long in a container so that the roots begin to coil round and round inside it
Root pruning	The removal of a part of a root system of a fruit tree to induce fruiting
Rootstock	The lower portion of a grafted plant
Rubbing out	The removal of shoots as they first start growing by rubbing the hand along the branch or trunk
Scion	The uppermost portion of a graft; the aerial part
Shoots	Usually a reference to young annual growths before they have started to lignify
Shrub	A woody plant that branches from near ground-level
Side shoots	Young growth other than the leaders
Silver leaf	A disease attacking a wide range of trees and shrubs, but particularly members of the rose family (Rosaceae), where the leaves take on a leaden or silvery appearance
Species roses	A rose which occurs in the wild as distinct from one which has arisen in cultivation
Sport	A plant propagated from, or a branch which develops on a tree or shrub differently from the rest in habit, size, shape, form or colour of foliage, flower or fruit
Spur	A restricted dwarf shoot system of fruit buds
Spur bearing	A fruit tree which produces its fruit on spurs
Standard	A tree having a clear stem of 1·8m (6ft) on top of which the branch system arises; 1·35m (4½ft) for roses
Stock	*see* Rootstock
Stool-like	The habit of shrubs where young stems are produced annually at or from beneath ground-level
Stopping	Removal of the growing tip to induce branching

Stub   The portion of a branch remaining when a branch has been cut off, but not flush with the trunk or the branch from which it arose.

Sub-laterals   Side shoots developing from a lateral

Sucker   A term with several meanings.
(a) A stem arising from the rootstock of a grafted plant
(b) A shoot emerging from damaged roots
(c) Shoots which emerge from below ground-level
(d) Young shoots developing along the trunk of some trees

Tap root   Main root

Terminal bud   The last growth bud produced in a growing season; the one at the end of a shoot

Tiered habit   Where the branch system develops naturally from the same point annually as in some conifers or where pairs of branches are trained to develop from selected positions along the trunk as when training espaliers

Tip bearers   Those varieties of apple tree that produce fruit buds on the tips of shoots instead of on spurs or laterals

Tipping   The removal of the tips of shoots when winter pruning

Topiary   Clipping of small trees or shrubs into ornamental or bizarre shapes

Tree   A woody plant having a clear stem of 1·8m (6ft) before branching

Triple cordon   A cordon in which there are three stems arising from low down on a single trunk, each clothed with fruit spurs

Truss   A metal tie used for supporting a large branch on an old tree

U cordon   A double stemmed cordon

Union   The point at which the scion and stock have united in a grafted plant

Unripe wood   Shoots in which the process of lignification is not complete by autumn

Water shoots   Soft sappy growth which develops from a trunk or within the mature framework of a tree

Whip   A single stem usually of one season's growth, either as a seedling or resulting from a grafted plant

Index